Landmark Historic U.S. Supreme Court Decisions

Landmarks:
Historic U.S. Supreme Court Decisions

Developed by
Marshall Croddy
Bill Hayes

Writers
Bill Hayes, Marshall Croddy, Carlton Martz,
Lucy Eisenberg, Erwin Chemerinsky, Hillary A. Bounds,
Yoni A. Fife, Coral Suter, and Paul Von Blum

Editor
Bill Hayes

Production & Design
Andrew Costly

CRF Board Reviewers
L. Rachel Helyar, Lisa M. Rockwell, Paul W.A. Severin,
K. Eugene Shutler, Gail Midgal Title, and Carlton Varner

Todd Clark, *Executive Director*
Marshall Croddy, *Director of Programs*
Constitutional Rights Foundation
601 South Kingsley Drive
Los Angeles, CA 90005
(213) 487-5590 • crf@crf-usa.org • www.crf-usa.org

Library of Congress Cataloging-in-Publication Data

Landmarks : historic U.S. Supreme Court decisions / writers, Bill Hayes ... [et al.].
    p. cm.
Includes bibliographical references.
ISBN 978-1-886253-42-1 (alk. paper)
1. Constitutional law—United States—Cases. 2. Constitutional history—United States—Cases. I. Hayes, Bill, 1945- II. Title.

KF4550.Z9L355 2007
342.73—dc22

2007032279

Landmarks:
Historic U.S. Supreme Court Decisions

Table of Contents

Preface

For this publication, Constitutional Rights Foundation was fortunate to be aided by a number of volunteers in addition to CRF staffers. We would like to thank them for taking time out of their busy schedules to contribute to CRF.

Lucy Eisenberg, Esq., has written numerous articles for CRF. For this volume, she contributed three articles:

> Inside the Marble Temple
>
> *Gideon v. Wainwright* (1963)
>
> *U.S. v. Nixon* (1974)

Two Associates at Skadden, Arps, Slate, Meagher & Flom LLP contributed articles:

> Hillary A. Bounds, Esq., wrote about *Gibbons v. Ogden* (1824).
>
> Yoni A. Fife, Esq., wrote on *Texas v. Johnson* (1989).

Erwin Chemerinsky is the Alston & Bird Professor of Law and Political Science at Duke University. He wrote on *Bush v. Gore* (2000).

All the volunteers agreed to give us complete editorial control. Thus any errors or mistakes are not theirs.

The remaining articles and all the questions and activities were written by CRF staff members, past and present, and by our longtime *Bill of Rights in Action* contributor Carlton Martz.

Inside the Marble Temple:
How the Supreme Court Works

The Supreme Court is the highest court in the land. Housed in a Roman-style temple, it overlooks both houses of Congress and the White House from its perch atop Capitol Hill in Washington, D.C. From October to late in April, the court hears oral argument on Mondays, Tuesdays and Wednesdays, and the press and the public are free to attend. But that is the only part of the court's decision-making open to public view. Otherwise, the court functions behind closed doors, in its marble temple on Capitol Hill.

Oyez, Oyez, Oyez

The Supreme Court's term begins each year on the first Monday in October. It holds oral argument for two consecutive weeks each month—as long as there are cases to decide—from October through April. At precisely 10 a.m., the marshal of the court calls the court to order, solemnly intoning:

> Oyez, oyez, oyez [a phrase from medieval England meaning "hear ye"]. The Honorable, the Chief Justice and the Associate Justices of the Supreme Court of the United States. All persons having business before this honorable Court are admonished to draw near and give their attention for the Court is now sitting. God save the United States and this honorable Court.

The nine justices, dressed in black robes, enter through a red velvet curtain in groups of three and take their seats behind a dark mahogany bench.

The names of the chief justice and eight associate justices are well known to the public. Nominated by the president, each must be confirmed by the U.S. Senate, often in televised proceedings. Political battles often break out over the confirmations, and the media covers them extensively.

After being confirmed, the justices "hold their Offices during good Behavior" (which means for life), and receive "a Compensation which shall not be diminished during their Continuance in Office" (U.S. Constitution, Article III, Section 1). That provision makes them essentially independent of Congress, the president, and the electorate. With life tenure, the justices can address the cases that come before the court without deferring to public opinion

Far less well known, and indeed generally unknown, are the law clerks. Each justice has four law clerks. Most of them serve for only one year. The clerks typically come to the court soon after finishing law school. Virtually all of them have clerked for a federal judge, but few have had experience in the practice of law or in public life. Yet they play an important role in the court process. They recommend which cases the court should hear, make suggestions about how the cases might be decided, and even prepare first drafts of the justices' opinions.

Also unknown are the almost 300 employees that keep the court running. The court, in the words of one reporter, is like a miniature city. The building houses a cafeteria, library, print shop,

Landmarks: Historic U.S. Supreme Court Decisions

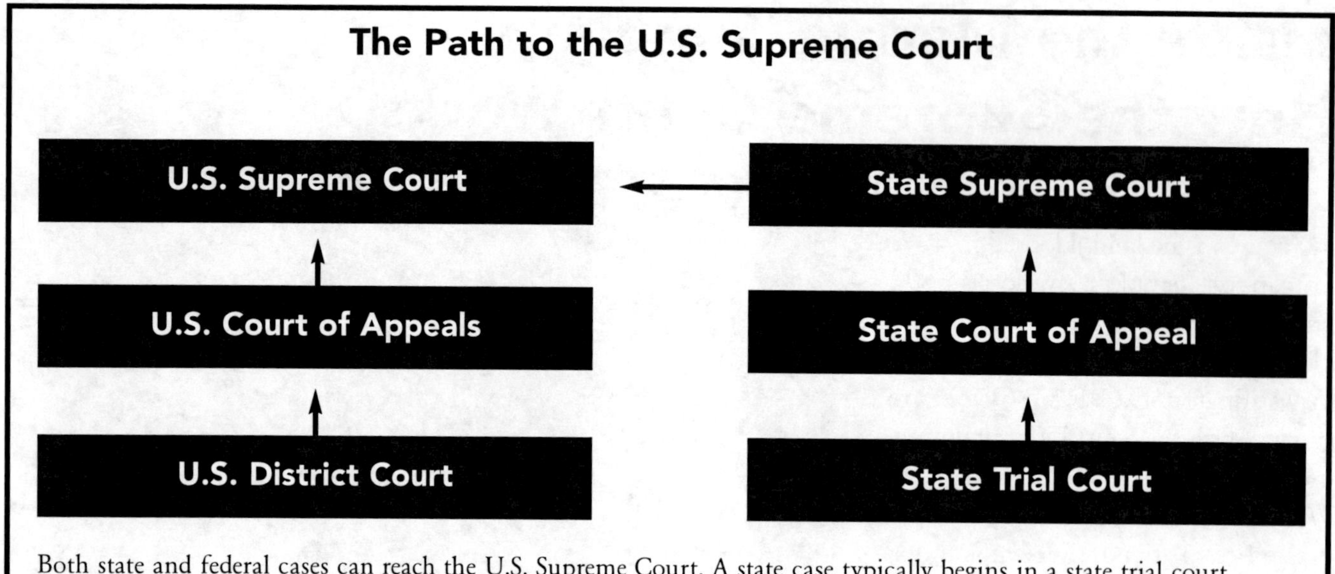

Both state and federal cases can reach the U.S. Supreme Court. A state case typically begins in a state trial court. It can be appealed to a state court of appeal (if the state has one) and then to the state's highest court (usually named the state supreme court). If the case presents a federal issue, an appeal can be made to the U.S. Supreme Court.

Federal cases typically begin in U.S. District Court, a trial court. They can be appealed to the U.S. Court of Appeals and then to the U.S. Supreme Court.

and gymnasium and basketball court. A seamstress, a nurse, carpenters, electricians, and 130 police officers work at the court. From the beginning of the workday until the end, the court's employees almost never leave the building.

Choosing Which Cases to Decide

Article III of the U.S. Constitution vests federal judicial power in the Supreme Court and in lower federal courts established by Congress. The courts only have power to decide cases between actual parties. The courts may not issue advisory opinions or create their own cases.

Like all federal courts, the Supreme Court may only decide questions of federal law or the U.S. Constitution. It interprets the meaning of federal statutes and the U.S. Constitution. It decides how federal law should be applied. It determines whether laws—state and federal—violate the U.S. Constitution. It may not, however, decide cases that do not present federal questions. Most cases—contract, divorce, tort, probate, property, even criminal—involve questions of state law. Such cases can only reach federal court if they somehow involve federal law or the U.S. Constitution.

The Supreme Court has what is known as original jurisdiction in certain cases, such as conflicts between states over shared borders or water rights. These cases originate in the Supreme Court, and the court is required to hear them. Such cases are rare, however, and when they occur, the court appoints a "master" to hear the evidence as a trial judge. The court then reviews the master's findings and decides the case.

Most of the time, the Supreme Court exercises appellate jurisdiction. Cases come to the Supreme Court when a party who has lost in a lower court petitions for a hearing. The request for a hearing is called a petition for writ of certiorari. (A writ is a court order. Certiorari is Latin meaning "to be informed of.") The petition requests the court to review the lower court's decision. When the court decides to hear the appeal, it issues a writ of certiorari. But in most cases, the request is denied. In 2004, 8,584 petitions for certiorari were filed, but only 80— fewer than 1 percent—were granted.

The petitions for a writ of certiorari fall into two categories. One is "paid cases" where the parties have paid the court's filing fee of $300 and filed 40 copies of all the required materials. The second group is *in forma pauperis* cases (the phrase is Latin for "in the form of a pauper"). These cases are brought by indigent people, most of whom are in state or federal prison. For them, the filing fee and the requirement for multiple copies are waived. The number of *in forma pauperis* petitions filed each year has increased dramatically in recent years. (In 1984, 2,416 *in forma pauperis* petitions were filed; in 2004 the number was 6,543). But few are granted. In 2004, only 11 pauper's petitions were accepted for full decisions on the merits.

The law clerks play an important role in deciding which cases to hear. After all the new petitions are distributed to the justices' chambers, the justices put the petitions in a "pool" and divide them among eight of the nine chambers. (Justice Stevens does not participate in the pool.) One law clerk is assigned to review each case and write a "pool memo," which summarizes the case and determines whether it is "certworthy"—i.e., whether it raises an issue that merits the court's attention. The pool memo is distributed to the other justices, who (in most cases) ask one of their clerks to review it and make an assessment of the case.

The final step in the screening process takes place at conferences held at the end of the summer and three times each month of the term. Justices vote to grant or deny review. Before a conference takes place, the chief justice reviews the pending petitions and makes a list of the cases that he believes should be discussed and voted on. This "discuss list" is circulated to the associate justices before the conference. If a justice feels that a case has been wrongly left off the list, the justice can ask that it be added. The rest of the cases are put on a so-called "dead list" and get no further

---

U.S. Supreme Court Rule 10
Considerations Governing Review on Certiorari

Review on a writ of certiorari is not a matter of right, but of judicial discretion. A petition for a writ of certiorari will be granted only for compelling reasons. The following, although neither controlling nor fully measuring the Court's discretion, indicate the character of the reasons the Court considers:

(a) a United States court of appeals has

   [i]   entered a decision in conflict with the decision of another United States court of appeals on the same important matter;

   [ii] has decided an important federal question in a way that conflicts with a decision by a state court of last resort; or

   [iii] has so far departed from the accepted and usual course of judicial proceedings, or sanctioned such a departure by a lower court, as to call for an exercise of this Court's supervisory power;

(b) a state court of last resort has decided an important federal question in a way that conflicts with the decision of another state court of last resort or of a United States court of appeals;

(c) a state court or a United States court of appeals has decided an important question of federal law that has not been, but should be, settled by this Court, or has decided an important federal question in a way that conflicts with relevant decisions of this Court.

A petition for a writ of certiorari is rarely granted when the asserted error consists of erroneous factual findings or the misapplication of a properly stated rule of law.

attention. (Of the average of 240 petitions scheduled for a regular conference, about 15 to 30 petitions will be discussed. The petitions that are not
discussed are denied without any recorded vote.)

The justices meet on Fridays at 8:30 a.m. in a
wood-paneled conference room in the chief justice's suite. After a ceremonial handshake, they
begin the discussion. The chief justice, or the justice who added a case to the discuss list, opens the
discussion and announces his vote. The rest of the
justices then speak in order of seniority (from senior to junior) and also announce their vote. By the
Rule of Four, four justices must vote to grant certiorari in order for the court to hear the case.

When the court accepts a case, it also decides
whether to require the parties to submit new
briefs (written agruments) and to hold oral argument or to give "summary consideration."
"Summary consideration" means that the court
will rely on the materials already submitted (in
the petition for certiorari and the response to the
petition). For summary-consideration cases, the
court may issue a short decision on the merits,
labeled "per curiam" and not signed by a justice.
("Per curiam" is Latin for "by the court.") Or it
may vacate the lower court's decision and send it
back to that court to reconsider.

During the last 10 years, the court has received a
total of approximately 8,000 cert petitions per
year, and it has granted a full review to fewer
than 90. How and why the justices decide which
cases to hear is rarely known. They meet in private, with no law clerks present. Criteria for
accepting cases are set forth in the court's Rule
10 (see this rule on page 7). One of the criteria is
a conflict between two lower courts—i.e., where a
court ruled on the same issue that had been
ruled on by another lower court and came to a
different result. Another criterion in Rule 10 is
the existence of important questions of federal
law that the court has not yet decided. But Rule
10 also emphasizes that ultimately the decision is
one for "judicial discretion." And the reasons the
justices decide to grant or deny cert are rarely
explained. Which four justices voted to hear a
case is not a matter of public record.

Occasionally, however, a justice who disagrees
with the decision not to hear a case may write a
dissent, setting forth reasons why the case raises
an issue that the court should address.

Oral Argument and Deciding Cases

If a petition for certiorari is granted review in
September or October, the case will usually be
scheduled for oral argument in January or
February. (A petition granted in June won't come
up until December). Before the argument, the
justices review the briefs filed by the parties. The
briefs must conform to precise rules regarding
length (no more than 50 pages), the type font,
and the format of the index. The rules even dictate the color of the cover: blue for the petitioner
(who seeks to overturn the lower court's judgment) and red for the respondent (who supports
the judgment of the lower court). In a large
majority of cases, "amicus curiae" briefs are filed.
They are limited to 30 pages and bound in a
green cover. (*Amicus curiae* is Latin for "friend of
the court.") Amicus briefs are filed by various
interest groups (such as trade associations, labor
unions, or groups like the American Civil
Liberties Union (ACLU) or the Heritage
Foundation. Filing an amicus brief gives interest
groups an opportunity to involve themselves in
the work of the court. Amicus briefs are common. Amicus briefs (in a gray cover) are also frequently filed by the U.S. solicitor general in cases
of interest to the government when it is not a
party. In the 1998 term, amicus briefs were filed
in more than 90 percent of the cases that were
decided on the merits, and in most cases, at least
four amicus briefs are filed.

The arguments in the briefs are supplemented by
the attorneys' presentations in oral argument.
With rare exception, oral argument is limited to
one-half hour for each party. (In *U.S. v. Nixon*, a
decision that ultimately led to President Nixon's
resignation, the parties were allowed three hours.)
The parties may also share part of their time with
the lawyer for an amicus. But generally the justices, not the lawyers, determine which issues are
addressed during oral argument. Indeed, it is rare

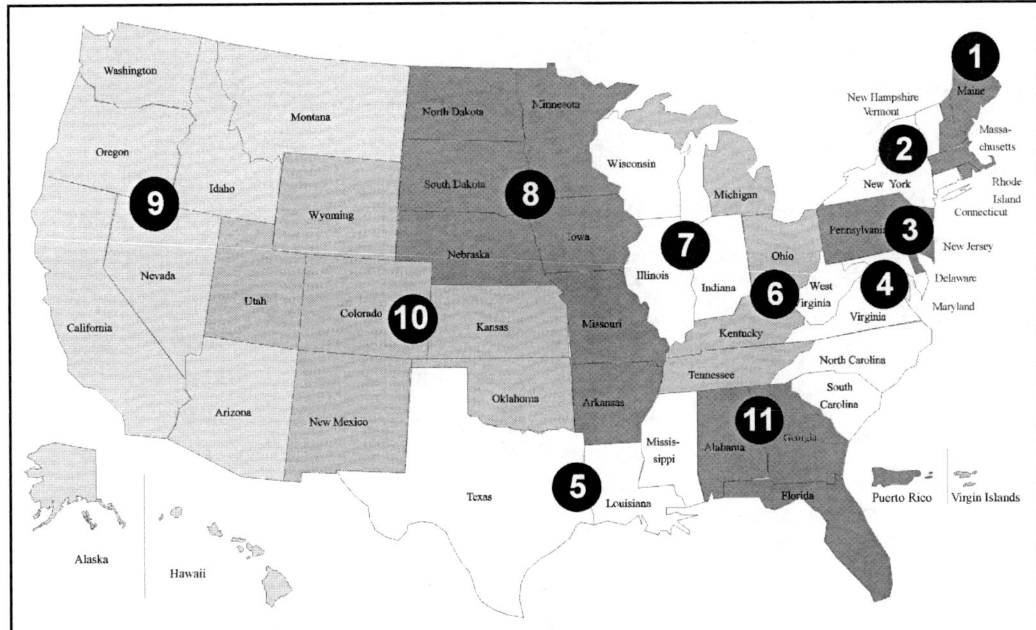

Geographic Boundaries of U.S. Courts of Appeals

The U.S. Courts of Appeals are divided into 12 circuits. The Courts of Appeals hear cases appealed from courts within their geographic area. The one exception is the Federal Circuit Court of Appeals. It hears appeals nationwide on specific issues, such as patent law.

for attorneys to be able to deliver their arguments as planned. Comparing the current day with the 1970s, Justice Ginsburg has said: ". . . then you could get at least five or six sentences out consecutively. Now we tend to interrupt not only counsel, but each other." Some lawyers believe that oral argument is irrelevant because the justices have already made up their minds before the hearing. But the justices disagree. In his book titled *The Supreme Court*, late Chief Justice Rehnquist stated: "I think it does make a difference: In a significant minority of the cases in which I have heard oral argument, I have left the bench feeling differently about a case than I did when I came on the bench."

Oral argument is heard on Monday, Tuesday, and Wednesday. On Friday mornings, the justices meet and discuss the cases argued that week. Again, the nine justices meet in private. No law clerks or secretaries are present. The discussion begins with the chief justice reviewing the facts, outlining his understanding of the issues and the applicable law, and indicating his or her vote (to affirm the decision of the lower court or reverse it). The eight associate justices speak, in order of seniority, and present their point of view and how they will vote. If it is a simple case with only one issue, it will be clear by the end of the conference that the majority has agreed on the basis

for either affirming or reversing the decision of the lower court.

The last step is to assign the task of preparing a written opinion that supports the result reached by the majority. The assignment is made by the chief justice—if he has voted with the majority—and if not, by the most senior associate justice who voted with the majority. Most justices assigned the task of writing an opinion will ask the clerk who has reviewed the case to prepare a first draft. The clerk will follow the justice's outline or suggestions. After the justice reviews and revises the draft, it is printed and distributed to the other justices. Others in the majority may accept the opinion as written or ask for changes. Whether or not the author of the opinion is willing to make changes may depend on how large the majority is. If only five justices voted in the majority, the opinion writer will try hard to satisfy critics to maintain five votes for the opinion. If the result at the conference was unanimous, the author will be much less likely to agree to substantial changes. Some opinions are revised a dozen or more times.

Most court opinions are not unanimous. In the 2004 term, the court was unanimous in 28 of its 76 cases. In some instances, a justice who agrees with the result may not agree with the reasoning of the author. That justice will issue a "concur-ring opinion." In other instances, a justice casts a dissenting vote, indicating disagreement with the result as it affects the parties in the case. When justices vote to dissent at the conference, there will be at least one, and perhaps multiple, dissenting opinions. The most senior justice among those dissenting will assign the task of writing the dissenting opinion. The justice writing the opinion may hope to persuade his colleagues to change their votes—to change a minority into a majority. That goal is rarely met. More often, the dissenting justices will be writing with the goal of influencing future cases and convincing the court to adopt their view.

Announcing the Decision

When the justices meet each Friday, the first order of business is to find out whether any cases have been finally decided. A case is finally decided when a version of each opinion has been drafted and each justice has decided which opinion to join. When this happens, the opinions will be announced in court the next week and copies made available for the public and the press. On the day of the announcement, the marshal proclaims "Oyez, oyez, oyez" and the court is convened. The first order of business is the announcement of the court's decision. The justice who authored the majority opinion will describe the case, explain the court's reasoning, and announce the result. The justice may also read a portion of the opinion. In unusually significant cases, the authors of dissenting opinions may also read from their opinions.

That ends the decision process. In the words of late Chief Justice Rehnquist, the process "has now run full circle. A case in which certiorari was granted somewhere from six months to a year ago has been briefed, orally argued, and now finally decided by the Supreme Court of the United States."

There is no appeal to a higher court. The U.S. Supreme Court is the highest court in the land. Its decisions set precedents binding on lower courts. When other courts are presented

questions of federal law or the U.S. Constitution, they must follow the rulings of the U.S. Supreme Court.

If Congress does not agree with the Supreme Court's interpretation of a federal law, it can change the law. But if it disagrees with the court's interpretation of the U.S. Constitution, it cannot change the court's interpretation by passing a law. There are just two ways of overruling a Supreme Court decision on the meaning of the Constitution. One, the Supreme Court in a subsequent decision may overrule itself. Two, the Constitution may be amended. If a decision is overruled, it is typically many years later.

All Supreme Court cases are important. They set precedents that other courts must follow. They are cases chosen from the thousands submitted to the court. Some Supreme Court cases decide issues of law that deeply affect American institutions and society. Known as landmarks, these decisions impact the history and future of the United States.

For Discussion

1. How are justices made independent of Congress, the president, and the electorate? Do you think they should be? Explain.

2. What do law clerks do? Of the things they do, which do you think is most important? Why?

3. What is a petition for writ of certiorari? Why do you think so few are granted? For what reasons do justices decide to grant certiorari? What is the Rule of Four?

4. What is a brief? What is an amicus curiae brief? Why do you think so many amicus briefs are filed with the court?

5. What is oral argument? Why do you think the court requires it? Do you think it is important? Explain.

6. Explain all the steps in the court's decision-making process. Which do you think is most important? Why?

ACTIVITY

Granting Certiorari

Your group is role playing members of the chambers of one of the nine Supreme Court justices. The court has received the petitions for certiorari summarized below. You must review these petitions. As a group, do the following:

1. Decide which member of your group will role play a Supreme Court justice. The rest of your group will role play law clerks working for the justice. The justice should lead your group's discussion.

2. Read each petition summary. For each petition summary, discuss and decide the following questions. To aid your discussion, review Rule 10 on page 7 and the section of the article titled "Choosing Which Cases to Decide" on pages 6–8:

   - Is the Supreme Court entitled to hear this case? Why or why not?

   - If so, should the Supreme Court grant certiorari? Why or why not?

3. Be prepared to discuss your conclusions and reasons for them.

Summary of Petitions for Writ of Certiorari

Petition 1: The petitioner, Sam Brown, is the police chief of a small city. The chief is planning to institute a policy of having city police officers ask for DNA samples of everyone they question. The program is voluntary, and people may refuse to give samples. The collected samples will be compiled into a database that can help solve crimes. Some members of the public have objected that this policy will violate the Fourth Amendment, which protects against unreasonable searches and seizures. The chief's petition for writ of certiorari asks for a hearing to determine if his proposed policy will violate the Fourth Amendment to the U.S. Constitution.

Petition 2: Petitioner, Amy Orange, was severely injured in a car accident. She sued the other driver in state court. The judge found that Orange was partially to blame for the accident and therefore could not collect under state law. Orange appealed to state appellate court and then to the state supreme court. Both ruled against her. She is petitioning for a hearing in the Supreme Court, claiming that the courts misinterpreted state law.

Petition 3: Petitioner Dan Green was convicted in state court of burglary. The jury that convicted him consisted of six members, which was the number set by state law. Green appealed the case to the state appeals court and state supreme court, losing in both courts. Green's petition for writ of certiorari claims that the state law, limiting the jury to six members, violates his right to a jury trial under the Sixth Amendment to the U.S. Constitution.

Petition 4: Petitioner Eva Red, a shareholder of stock in Giganto Company, Inc., sued its chief executive for securities fraud, claiming the statements he made about the stock were false and caused her to lose money. She sued under a federal law that required she allege facts showing a "strong inference" that the chief executive knew his statements were false. The federal trial court dismissed the case because it said she failed to allege facts amounting to a "strong inference." The Court of Appeals upheld the trial court's ruling, saying that a "strong inference" required that the inference be at least as compelling as any inference of innocence that could be drawn from the facts. The petitioner has petitioned for a writ of certiorari, pointing out that the Courts of Appeal are split on what "strong inference" means. Other Courts of Appeal have ruled that it means simply that a reasonable person could infer from the facts that the chief executive knew the statements were false. This standard, the petitioner argues, is the correct one.

Marbury v. Madison (1803)
The First Case of Judicial Review

James Madison (1751–1836) was one of the most important founders of the United States. He was one of the main authors of the Constitution, wrote many of the *Federalist Papers*, drafted the Bill of Rights, and went on to be the fourth U.S. president. He was also the defendant in one of the most significant Supreme Court cases, *Marbury v. Madison*.

"Who shall I nominate now?" President John Adams turned thoughtfully to his secretary of state. Adams was trying to find a new chief justice of the United States. The man he counted on to take the post had declined the honor.

The president's question stymied Secretary John Marshall, a lanky, somewhat awkward ex-Congressman from Virginia. He had been on the job only six months. Though a popular lawyer—a legal genius, some said—he had no idea who should fill the nation's highest judicial post. Maybe the president should consider someone already on the Supreme Court. What about Associate Justice Patterson?

"I shall not nominate him," said the President decidedly. He paused a moment, then looked at Marshall. "I believe I must nominate you."

Abrupt as it may seem, Adams' choice was sound. He needed a chief justice who shared his firm Federalist views and would fight for a strong central government. Marshall was such a jurist. And Adams had to act quickly: He was about to lose his job.

A few months before, in the fall of 1800, voters had rejected the Federalist vision of rule by "the rich, the good and the wise." Thomas Jefferson's Democratic Republican Party, which favored rule by "the people," won control of Congress and the presidency. On March 4, 1801, Adams would hand his young nation over to a group that Federalists feared would destroy it. When John Marshall became chief justice in early February, Adams knew he had at least slowed the Democratic Republicans down.

Marshall was not Adams' only last-minute jurist. At 9 p.m. on March 3, three hours before the Democratic Republicans took office, Adams appointed 42 new justices of the peace and rushed their papers to the Senate. Under Federalist control until midnight, it had stayed in session just to confirm these appointments. John Marshall, in his role as secretary of state, signed the documents. But before the commissions were delivered, the clock ran out.

Thomas Jefferson, the new president, did not want more Federalist officials. In any case, he doubted that Adams' last acts were legally binding. He told his secretary of state, James Madison, to withhold 17 of the undelivered commissions. With no official papers, the 17 Federalists would not get their appointments.

There the matter would have ended, except that four of the men awaiting appointments seemed to want theirs badly. In 1789, Congress had passed a law, the Judiciary Act, giving the Supreme Court power to issue writs of mandamus. These legal orders, which get their name from Latin meaning "we command," allow courts to tell government officials to take particular actions. The four job-seekers, one of them named William Marbury, asked the Supreme Court for a writ of mandamus ordering Secretary of State Madison to deliver the 17 commissions left over from Adams' term.

Marbury's request put Chief Justice Marshall in a difficult spot. If the Supreme Court ordered Madison to deliver Marbury's papers, the secretary would surely refuse to obey. Jefferson and the Democratic Republican Congress would back him.

With no way to enforce its order, Marshall's court could do little about Madison's disobedience. The court's power, and with it Federalist influence in the coming years, would be endangered.

Of course, Marshall could turn Marbury down. But refusing the writ would cast doubt on the legality of Adams' last-minute actions. People would accuse the court of ignoring the law or of evading it to appease the Democratic Republicans. Whatever the court did, it was bound to lose prestige.

But John Marshall found a way out. His solution is still a high point in American legal reasoning. First, he said, Marbury's appointment was perfectly legal, and he should get his papers. If Madison wouldn't deliver them, Marbury had every right to demand a writ of mandamus.

But—and here's the twist—the Supreme Court could not give Marbury his writ because it had no constitutional authority to do so. Indeed, Congress had no constitutional authority to grant the Supreme Court power to issue such writs. In short, Marshall ruled that the court must give up the power of issuing writs of mandamus because part of the Judiciary Act of 1789 was unconstitutional.

Jefferson despised the ruling because it affirmed Marbury's claims and Adams' actions. But there was nothing the president could do. Since he had not received an order, he could not embarrass the court by refusing to obey. By giving up the small power of issuing writs of mandamus, the court established a great power: judicial review. Judicial review allows courts to examine laws and executive acts and, if they violate the Constitution, overrule them.

Marshall's decision gave the court a power not explicitly granted it in the Constitution. In doing this, Marshall followed the lead of Federalist framers like Alexander Hamilton who expected the courts to protect private rights from Congress. Marshall's ruling set a precedent that state and federal judges have followed ever since. Judicial review is now key to our government's system of checks and balances.

The court did not declare another act of Congress unconstitutional until the *Dred Scott* case, 54 years later. Oddly enough, one man controlled the court for much of the intervening half century. That man was John Marshall. And *Marbury v. Madison* was but the first of dozens of his controversial and important opinions.

For Discussion

1. Who was John Marshall?

2. Who was William Marbury? What did he want? What was *Marbury v. Madison* about?

3. Was Marshall's *Marbury v. Madison* decision fair? How would you have decided the case? Why?

4. As Adams' secretary of state, Marshall took part in the events that led to *Marbury v. Madison*. Should he have excused himself from the case? If a judge played a similar role in a case today, would his or her decision be suspect? Explain.

5. What is judicial review? If the courts lacked this power, what might happen when Congress or the president violated the Constitution?

6. Who do you think should have the final say about what the Constitution means: the courts, the president, or Congress? Explain.

ACTIVITY

Jurisdiction

Article III of the U.S. Constitution lays out the powers of the U.S. Supreme Court. Its Section 2 lists the different kinds of cases the federal courts are allowed to resolve. The second paragraph of Section 2 explains which cases must be started (must "originate") in the Supreme Court itself and which reach the Supreme Court only on appeal from lower courts.

As a group, review the Constitution's Article III, Section 2, on the opposite page. For each of the four cases described below, discuss and decide the following questions:

1. Can the case be tried in federal courts? Why or why not?

2. If it can be tried in federal court, does the Supreme Court have original or appellate jurisdiction over the case? Why?

Base your decisions on the Constitution's Article III, Section 2, on the opposite page.

Cases

A. The owner of a fast-food stand in Denver signed a one-year contract with an Idaho-based supplier of frozen french fries. Six months later, claiming the food arrived late and was sometimes spoiled, she refused to accept or pay for further shipments. Her supplier says she owes him $512,000 and takes her to court for breaking the contract.

B. A man owed his ex-wife $1,800 in child-support payments. When he won $1,000 in his state's lottery, the government withheld the money to pay his debt. He feels this is not fair and sues to get the money back.

C. A foreign dictator used his country's public money to buy Florida real estate. When he fell from power, the new government claimed he acted illegally. It now wants the state of Florida to give it title to the property and sues Florida to accomplish this goal.

D. Members of a church in Texas are charged with breaking immigration laws by harboring illegal aliens. They claim the aliens are political refugees whom the federal government will not acknowledge because it supports tyrannical regimes in their homelands.

U.S. Constitution
Article III, Section 2

This section of the U.S. Constitution spells out which matters are for federal courts to decide (the jurisdiction of the federal courts). It also lays out when the Supreme Court has original jurisdiction (when it acts as a trial court) and when it has appellate jurisdiction (when it reviews the decisions of lower courts). The text of this section has not been changed, but its clauses have been separated and numbered for clarity.

[Jurisdiction of the Federal Courts]

The judicial power shall extend

[1] to all cases, in law and equity, arising under this Constitution, the laws of the United States, and treaties made, or which shall be made, under their authority;

[2] to all cases affecting ambassadors, other public ministers and consuls;

[3] to all cases of admiralty and maritime jurisdiction;

[4] to controversies to which the United States shall be a party;

[5] to controversies

    [A] between two or more states;

    [B] between a state and citizens of another state;

    [C] between citizens of different states;

    [D] between citizens of the same state claiming lands under grants of different states . . .

    [E] between a state, or the citizens thereof, and foreign states, citizens or subjects.

[Original or Appellate Jurisdiction]

In all cases affecting ambassadors, other public ministers and consuls, and those in which a state shall be party, the Supreme Court shall have original jurisdiction. In all the other cases before mentioned, the Supreme Court shall have appellate jurisdiction, both as to law and fact, with such exceptions, and under such regulations as the Congress shall make.

. . .

McCulloch v. Maryland (1819)

John Marshall and the Bank Case

Located in Philadelphia, Pennsylvania, the building of the second Bank of the United States is today part of Independence National Historical Park.

[The Constitution is] intended to endure for ages to come, and consequently, to be adapted to the various crises of human affairs.

—Chief Justice John Marshall in *McCulloch v. Maryland* (1819)

What sort of government should the United States have? This question faced the writers of the Constitution in 1787. The Articles of Confederation, the first national government, had left almost all power to the states. Most viewed the Confederation a failure. Many believed that to continue leaving government power in the hands of the states would cripple the infant nation. Others repeatedly voiced their fears about a centralized government controlled by a few all-powerful men. Those who wrote the Constitution attempted to resolve these concerns.

The Constitution was ratified only after promises were made that a bill of rights would be added to it. When the First Congress met, it drafted the Bill of Rights. One amendment in particular addressed the concerns of those who worried the new national government would obliterate the powers of the states. The 10th Amendment stated, "The powers not delegated to the United States by the Constitution, nor prohibited by it to the states, are reserved to the states respectively, or to the people."

Even after the Bill of Rights was ratified in 1791, doubts remained about just what powers the U.S. government could exercise. Sooner or later, the U.S. Congress was bound to pass a law that the states would claim went beyond the constitutional powers of the national government. When Congress chartered the second Bank of the United States in 1816, the stage was set for a monumental clash between Congress and the states. The controversy was played out before the U.S. Supreme Court in the case of *McCulloch v. Maryland*. Chief Justice John Marshall wrote the unanimous court decision. In the words of Marshall's biographer, this decision "so decisively influenced the growth of the nation that, by many, it is considered as only second in importance to the Constitution itself."

A Tax on the Bank

In 1791, Alexander Hamilton successfully argued to establish a privately owned national bank. Chartered by Congress, the bank facilitated the financial transactions of the U.S. government. The charter of this first Bank of the United States extended only to 1811 and was not renewed. After the War of 1812, however, the finances of the U.S. government were in shambles. This situation prompted efforts to restore the national bank.

Congress created a second Bank of the United States in 1816, but financial problems continued to plague the country. The bank seemed to add to these troubles. It was mismanaged, and radical swings in its interest rates hurt many competing state banks. On top of this, bank officers were found to be using depositors' money to buy and sell bank stock. Many Americans, especially in the South and West, concluded that the bank was causing the economic depression ravaging the country.

Some states attempted to retaliate against the "monster monopoly." They either banned the bank outright or taxed it. In February 1818, Maryland passed a law requiring a stamp tax on all notes issued by banks not chartered by the state. In May of the same year, Maryland sued James W. McCulloch, an officer of the Baltimore branch of the Bank of the United States. Technically, McCulloch was sued for $110, the penalty for circulating unstamped banknotes in violation of Maryland's tax law. Everyone on both sides of the case, however, knew that a great deal more was at stake.

McCulloch v. Maryland

Maryland won its case in the state courts, but the bank appealed to the U.S. Supreme Court. The Supreme Court consisted then of seven justices. The chief justice was John Marshall, a Virginia Federalist. Most of the other justices were Democratic Republicans, who normally would be expected to decide cases in favor of states' rights.

Arguments on the case began February 22, 1819. Three lawyers represented each side. Among those speaking on behalf of the bank was Daniel Webster, who was just beginning to build his reputation as a great orator and statesman. The other side included Luther Martin, who was the attorney general for Maryland. He had been a delegate to the Constitutional Convention in 1787.

The case centered around two constitutional questions. First, did Congress have the constitutional power to create a nationally chartered bank? Second, did Maryland (and other states) have the constitutional power to tax a national bank chartered by Congress?

The oral arguments before the Supreme Court went back and forth for nine days. On the first question, the attorneys representing Maryland pointed out that chartering banks was not one of the "delegated powers" of Congress. Those powers are listed in Article I, Section 8, of the Constitution. Among the listed powers are collecting taxes, borrowing money, and regulating commerce. But setting up a bank is not listed. Where then, the attorneys asked, did Congress get its authority to set up the Bank of the United States? The Maryland attorneys argued that unless a power was specifically granted to Congress in the Constitution, it remained with the states.

Luther Martin drove home this point: "We insist, that the only safe rule is the plain letter of the Constitution, the rule . . . in the Tenth Amendment . . . that the powers not delegated to the United States nor prohibited to the states, are reserved to the states respectively, or to the people." Martin concluded that therefore only the states, or the people they represent, had the power to incorporate banks.

Landmarks: Historic U.S. Supreme Court Decisions

Marshall's Opinion

On March 6, 1819, barely three days after the last oral argument in *McCulloch v. Maryland*, Chief Justice John Marshall announced the Supreme Court's unanimous decision. The court ruled in favor of the bank and against the right of the states to tax it. The opinion of the court, written by Marshall, was nothing less than a justification for congressional or national power at the expense of the states.

In any conflict between national and state power, wrote Marshall, a law passed by Congress "is supreme within its sphere of action." Did Congress have the constitutional power to establish a national bank in the first place? Yes, said Marshall, Congress has the power to pass all laws "necessary and proper" to carry out its delegated powers in Article I, Section 8, of the Constitution. The bank provided the means to carry out these powers. Therefore, the act of Congress chartering the bank "is a law made in pursuance of the Constitution, and is part of the supreme law of the land."

On the second question about whether Maryland had the power to tax the bank, Marshall ruled it did not. He declared that states can only tax their own people and property. The bank was an "instrument" of the U.S. government, which represents all the people. If Maryland were allowed to tax the bank, he argued, this might lead to taxes on other U.S. government operations. Marshall repeated Webster's warning that "the power to tax involves the power to destroy." The result would be a crippled national government bowing "at the foot of the states." Marshall concluded by saying that "the states have no power, by taxation or otherwise, to retard, burden, or in any manner control the operations of the constitutional laws enacted by Congress."

In effect, Marshall and the other justices of the Supreme Court reduced the power of the states in two ways. First, by activating the "necessary and proper" clause, the court expanded the potential for congressional lawmaking. Second, by invalidating Maryland's stamp tax on the

John Marshall (1755–1835) held the office of chief justice of the U.S. Supreme Court longer than any other justice (1801–1835). His decisions helped shape the meaning the U.S. Constitution.

Speaking for Congress and the bank, Daniel Webster referred the justices to another part of the Constitution. In the last paragraph of Article I, Section 8, Congress is given the power "to make all Laws which shall be necessary and proper" to carry out its delegated powers. "A bank is a proper and suitable instrument to assist the operations of the government," Webster concluded.

Concerning the second question of the case, the attorneys representing Maryland noted that the Constitution placed no limit on the power of a state to tax any person or property within its borders. Daniel Webster responded by asking, "If the states may tax the bank, to what extent shall they tax it, and where shall they stop?" Webster wondered if states would go on to tax the mail or perhaps even the U.S. courts. He warned, "An unlimited power to tax involves, necessarily, a power to destroy . . . ."

bank, the justices eliminated state taxation as a means of undermining acts of Congress.

The decision of the Supreme Court and Marshall's written opinion were bitterly attacked, particularly in the South and West. Thomas Jefferson called the Supreme Court justices "a subtle corps of sappers and miners constantly working underground to undermine the foundations of our constitutional fabric." The criticism was so intense that John Marshall, writing as "A Friend of the Constitution" defended the decision in a series of letters to a Philadelphia newspaper. Ohio continued the controversy for another five years in a lawsuit over that state's confiscation of bank funds.

In the end, however, Marshall and the Supreme Court prevailed. Marshall's broad view of national power gradually overshadowed the 10th Amendment and the idea that Congress could act only on those powers specifically mentioned in the Constitution. Albert Beveridge, the biographer of John Marshall, has written that the chief justice made the Constitution "a living thing, capable of growth, capable of keeping pace with the advancement of the American people and ministering to their changing necessities."

For Discussion

1. Why was the Bank of the United States controversial?

2. How did Maryland attempt to restrict the power of the bank?

3. What two constitutional issues did the court decide in *McCulloch v. Maryland*?

4. What were the arguments on each issue?

5. What was the decision of the court? Do you agree with it? Why or why not?

6. Why was it surprising that the decision was unanimous? What did Daniel Webster and John Marshall mean when they said that "the power to tax involves the power to destroy"?

7. Why was the decision important?

'Necessary and Proper'

In *McCulloch v. Maryland*, the U.S. Supreme Court ruled that Congress had the authority to charter a national bank based on the "necessary and proper" clause of the Constitution. In later years, this "implied power" enabled Congress to pass laws in many different areas.

Imagine that you are a group of constitutional scholars. As a group, do the following:

1. Read and discuss Article I, Section 8, of the Constitution and the 10th Amendment of the Bill of Rights.

2. Decide which of the proposals listed below Congress has the authority under Article I, Section 8, to establish or regulate. (You are not deciding whether any of these proposals are a good or bad idea. Your job, as constitutional scholars, is to advise whether or not they are constitutional and why.)

3. Be prepared to report your decisions and reasons for each of them.

Proposals

1. a national sales tax

2. a national property tax

3. a ban on the sale of cigarettes

4. a schedule of fares for all airlines

5. a system of rationing gasoline

6. a national lottery

7. a nationally funded healthcare program

8. a national curriculum for all public schools

9. a ban on the sale of handguns

10. a military draft for men and women

Gibbons v. Ogden (1824)

The Meaning of the Commerce Clause

The case of *Gibbons v. Ogden* involved a dispute over who had the right to transport passengers on steamboats between New York and New Jersey.

The Congress shall have Power . . . To regulate Commerce with foreign Nations, and among the several States, and with the Indian Tribes.
—Commerce Clause, Article I, Section 8, U.S. Constitution

In 1808, the state of New York granted a monopoly to operate steamboats on the state's waters, including the waters between New York and its neighboring states. The federal government, however, had issued a federal coasting license to Thomas Gibbons. This license allowed him to operate steamboats between the states of New York and New Jersey. The federal license conflicted with the license held by Aaron Ogden under the New York monopoly. Ogden filed a complaint asking the New York Court of Chancery to shut down Gibbons' operation between New York and New Jersey.

The Court of Chancery found in favor of Ogden. It issued an injunction forcing Gibbons to stop operating his steamboats in the waters between New York and New Jersey. Gibbons appealed the case to the Court of Errors of New York. The Court of Errors affirmed the lower court decision. Gibbons then appealed to the U.S. Supreme Court.

The case involved the meaning of the commerce clause of the U.S. Constitution. Found in Article I, Section 8, the clause reads:

> The Congress shall have Power . . . To regulate Commerce with foreign Nations, and among the several States, and with the Indian Tribes.

The first government of the United States did not give Congress this power. Created by the Articles of Confederation during the American Revolution, the articles severely limited the power of the central government. The power to regulate trade was left to the individual states. This grant of power to the states led to confusion and problems in transactions between states and with other nations. These problems, among others, led to the drafting of the Constitution.

Ogden's attorney made two arguments. First, he argued that the Constitution's commerce clause did not give Congress exclusive power over interstate commerce. He contended that states also had this power. He pointed out the federal and the state governments shared powers in many areas, such as the ability to levy taxes.

Second, Odgen's attorney argued that Congress did not have power under the commerce clause to regulate Gibbons' boats because he was not engaged in commerce. He was transporting passengers, not goods or "trade."

The Supreme Court's Decision

Chief Justice John Marshall delivered the opinion of the Supreme Court. His decision rejected Ogden's arguments and ruled in favor of Gibbons. Marshall's opinion effectively spoke on the greater issue of Congress' power over the national economy.

First, he addressed Odgen's argument that he was not engaged in commerce. Marshall defined the term "commerce" as used in the Constitution. He found that commerce includes navigation because that is the common understanding of the word. He went on to state that commerce encompasses anything that is "commercial intercourse." Therefore, although the ferry was only carrying passengers instead of commercial goods, it was still involved in commerce. This broad definition has helped justify subsequent congressional acts that may seem outside the traditional view of commerce.

Marshall went on to define the phrase "among the several states." He concluded that commerce among the states meant anything that was not fully contained within a single state. That meant the federal government could regulate any good unless it was entirely made, sold, and used within one state. Therefore, regulation could extend to the interior of the state and was not confined to transactions at the state's borders.

Next, Marshall's decision dealt with whether Congress shared the power to regulate interstate commerce with the states. Marshall concluded that the framers of the Constitution intended Congress to establish uniform regulation of trade. Therefore, the states did not share the power to regulate interstate commerce. Marshall noted that the only limits to the congressional power to regulate commerce are those prescribed by the Constitution itself.

The primary motive of Marshall's decision was to establish the Constitution as a functional document. He believed that strictly interpreting the powers vested in Congress would make the Constitution "unfit for use." Marshall could have written a brief decision holding for Gibbons and allowing him to operate his steamboats. Instead, he took this opportunity to broadly define the powers of Congress and ultimately vest the federal government with the ability to create a strong and efficient economy. Marshall's ability to foresee the benefits of an economy centrally controlled by the Congress rather than by the competing economic policies of the states is one of the most enduring principles from his time on the Supreme Court.

Commerce Clause Interpretation Since *Gibbons v. Ogden*

The Marshall court's expansive interpretation of the commerce clause did not end the debates over its meaning. In different eras, Congress has tried to pass various legislation, using the commerce clause as a justification for the legislation. Its efforts have often been challenged in court, and the Supreme Court has ruled on the commerce clause. The court's rulings have depended on the changing philosophies of the justices, the politics of the era, and the circumstances of the cases.

The next major test of the commerce clause came in 1895. It involved a lawsuit brought under the Sherman Antitrust Act. Passed in 1890, this act made it illegal for businesses to monopolize or restrain interstate commerce. The federal government filed an injunction to prevent the merger of five sugar manufacturing companies. Combined, the companies would account for 98 percent of the nation's sugar refineries. In *U.S. v. E.C. Knight Company*, the Supreme Court ruled 8-1 against the government. The court held that manufacturing was a local activity, and therefore Congress had no power under the commerce clause to regulate it. The court concluded that only the states, not the federal government, could regulate manufacturing. The lone dissenter argued that inflated prices would affect interstate commerce, but the majority contended that it was merely an "indirect" effect and would exceed the scope of the power granted to Congress in the Constitution.

The Supreme Court further restricted the commerce clause with its 1918 5-4 decision in *Hammer v. Dagenhart*. This case challenged the Federal Child Labor Act, which barred shipping across state lines any goods made with child labor. The court held that Congress was over-reaching its powers since the goods were produced using child labor within the state and posed no threat to the nation's economy after their production.

After the Great Depression shattered the U.S. economy in the 1930s, President Franklin D. Roosevelt moved many bills through Congress in an attempt to aid national recovery. These bills required an expansive interpretation of the commerce clause, and the Supreme Court upheld many of these acts. But two important initiatives were successfully challenged in court.

The Supreme Court struck down the National Industry Recovery Act in *Schechter Poultry v. U.S.* (1935). The act authorized the president to approve codes of fair competition developed by industry boards. In this case, the court declared unconstitutional the Live Poultry Code, which mandated wages, hours, and industry trade practices. The court considered the plight of the national economy in its decision, but stated that "extraordinary circumstances do not create or enlarge constitutional power." The court held that the code's regulations went beyond interstate commerce and encompassed practices concerning even the sale and slaughter of the chicken in local slaughterhouses.

The next important piece of legislation the court struck down was the Coal Conservation Act. The act set up a system of local coal boards with the power to set minimum prices and granted employees the right to organize and bargain collectively. The Supreme Court by a 5-4 vote in *Carter v. Carter Coal Co.* (1936) determined that the labor provisions in the statute overstepped the power granted to Congress in the commerce clause. The court stated that the word "commerce" meant "intercourse for the purposes of trade." It concluded that the mining of coal did not fit this definition. "The employment of men, the fixing of their wages, hours of labor and working conditions, the bargaining in respect of these things . . . constitute intercourse for the purposes of production, not of trade."

These Supreme Court decisions angered President Roosevelt. Re-elected in a landslide victory in 1936, Roosevelt proposed new legislation granting him the power to appoint more judges to the Supreme Court. Such a law would have allowed him to pack the court with justices who supported him. Before Congress acted on the legislation, one justice switched sides in the commerce clause debate. In *NLRB v. Jones & Laughlin Steel Corp.*

The legislative program of Franklin Delano Roosevelt, U.S. president from 1933–1945, depended on an expansive view of the U.S. Constitution's commerce clause.

(1937), the court upheld the National Labor Relations Act, which granted employees the right to organize and collectively bargain. This historic case later came to be known as "the switch in time that saved nine," referring to the number of justices sitting on the Supreme Court. (After this decision, Roosevelt's court-packing legislation died in the Senate.) The decision noted that laws protecting employees had proven to have positive results on interstate commerce. The court concluded that even activities "intrastate in character when separately considered" may be regulated "if they have such a close and substantial relation to interstate commerce that their control is essential or appropriate to protect that commerce from burdens and obstructions . . . ."

After this decision, the Supreme Court continued to take an expansive view of the commerce clause. Congress often used the commerce clause as a basis for important social initiatives. For example, the Civil Rights Act of 1964 was based on the commerce clause. The act prohibited businesses from discriminating against customers on the basis of race, color, religion, sex, or national origin. The law was challenged and brought before the Supreme Court in *Heart of Atlanta Motel v. U.S.* (1964). A unanimous court upheld the law. (Two justices filed concurring opinions.) The court connected a hotel serving primarily local customers to interstate commerce by emphasizing the role hotels have in allowing people to be mobile and travel across state lines. The court further cited the hotel's advertisements in other locations as evidence of its place outside the local community. The court acknowledged that Congress was primarily addressing a moral issue with the statute, but evidence also showed that interstate commerce was disrupted by discriminatory policies practiced by hotels. In *Katzenbach v. McClung* (1964), the court further expanded the scope of interstate commerce. It upheld applying the Civil Rights Act to a local restaurant because it served food previously transported over state lines. The court pointed out that the business of this single restaurant may not significantly impact interstate commerce, but the court stated that the impact of all restaurants in similar circumstances had to be considered.

These and other cases seemed to indicate the Supreme Court's full support of the increasing congressional authority claimed under the commerce clause. No major challenges were heard by the court until 1995. By that time, however, another political shift had occurred. In two major decisions, a 5–4 court majority signaled a movement toward a more restrictive interpretation of the commerce clause. First, in *U.S. v. Lopez* (1995), the court struck down the Gun-Free School Zones Act. This law imposed strict penalties for possession of firearms within 1,000 feet of a school zone. The court stated that Congress only had the power to regulate three broad areas: (1) the channels of interstate commerce, (2) the instrumentalities of interstate commerce or persons and things in interstate commerce, and (3) activities with a substantial relation to or that substantially affect interstate commerce. The court further clarified its position in *U.S. v. Morrison* (2000) by holding the Violence Against Women Act, establishing civil remedies for victims of gender-motivated crime, unconstitutional. Chief Justice Rehnquist writing for the majority stated that for Congress to regulate an intrastate activity, it must be economic in nature. He argued that if this type of statute were allowed, then Congress could regulate any crime as long as the national impact of the crime substantially affected employment, production, transit, or consumption.

• • • • •

The commerce clause grants power to Congress to regulate many aspects of the national economy. This power is checked by the Supreme Court's interpretation of the Constitution. Beginning with the landmark *Gibbons v. Ogden* decision, the court has struggled to balance the interests of the federal system of government with the desire of Congress to enact nationwide solutions to both economic and social challenges faced by the country. In some eras, the court has taken an expansive view of the commerce clause. In others, it has taken a more restrictive view.

For Discussion

1. How is the Constitution's commerce clause different from the power given by the Articles of Confederation? Why do you think the framers of the Constitution made it different?

2. What were the facts of the case in *Gibbons v. Ogden*? What two arguments did Ogden's attorney make in the case? What was the decision of the Supreme Court? What were the court's reasons for its decision?

3. The Supreme Court in *Gibbons v. Ogden* gave an expansive reading of the commerce clause. Other courts have given it a more restrictive reading. Why do you think this has happened? Which reading do you think is correct? Why?

ACTIVITY

Revisiting Commerce Cases

Imagine that you are members of John Marshall's Supreme Court, and you are going to decide one of the commerce clause cases decided by subsequent courts. Your teacher will assign your group one (or more) of the cases below:

a. *U.S. v. E.C. Knight Company*

b. *Hammer v. Dagenhart*

c. *Schechter Poultry v. U.S.*

d. *Carter v. Carter Coal Co.*

e. *NLRB v. Jones & Laughlin Steel Corp.*

f. *Heart of Atlanta Motel v. U.S.*

g. *Katzenbach v. McClung*

h. *U.S. v. Lopez*

i. *U.S. v. Morrison*

As a group, do the following:

1. Read and discuss the commerce clause and the *Gibbons v. Ogden* decision described in the article. You will base your decision in the other case on this decision.

2. Read and discuss your assigned case.

3. Decide this case on the principles announced in *Gibbons v. Ogden*.

4. Discuss and decide what you think the decision of the court should have been in this case.

5. Be prepared to announce your decisions and your reasons for them to the whole class.

Dred Scott v. Sandford (1857)

Slavery and the Constitution

This political cartoon was published during the election of 1860. It depicts Dred Scott playing a fiddle while each of the four presidential candidates dances. Clockwise from the upper left are candidates John C. Breckinridge, Abraham Lincoln, John Bell, and Stephen A. Douglas.

The *Dred Scott* case was decided three years before the Civil War began. Decided by a court dominated by pro-slavery justices, the case helped propel the nation into war.

Dred Scott was a slave belonging to John Emerson, an Army doctor, who lived in St. Louis, Missouri. When the Army transferred Emerson, Emerson took his slave with him. First, they went to Fort Armstrong in Illinois and then in 1836 to Fort Snelling, an outpost in the Minnesota Territory.

At Fort Snelling, Dred Scott met Harriet Robinson, a teenager imported from Virginia. Her owner, unlike many whites, believed in legal marriage for slave couples. After Dred and Harriet were married, the young woman's owner gave her to Dr. Emerson so she could live with her husband.

The next year, Emerson was transferred to Louisiana. He left the Scotts behind, but sent for them when he got married to a woman named Irene Sanford. Within six months, the two families returned to Fort Snelling. Traveling upriver on steamboat, Harriet bore a child, Eliza.

Eliza was 18 months old when the Army sent Emerson to Florida. His wife took the slaves to her father's home in St Louis and hired them out to work for others. The doctor returned two years later,

Landmarks: Historic U.S. Supreme Court Decisions

left the Scotts to produce income in St. Louis, and took his wife to Iowa. She gave birth to a child, and Dr. Emerson died a short time later.

Mrs. Emerson inherited the Scotts from her husband. Returning to St. Louis, she rented them to her brother-in-law, a colonel. The slaves were living at the local barracks in 1845 when their second daughter, Lizzy, was born. In March 1846, Irene Emerson hired the Scotts to Samuel Russell and his wife. A few days later, Dred Scott took Irene Emerson to court. He claimed that he and his family were free.

Nobody knows why he did it. Years later, one reporter said that Emerson refused to let him buy his family's freedom. Another thought she was about to sell Eliza and Lizzy out of state. One of his lawyers said Scott simply didn't like being hired out to different people all the time. He never stated his reasons in public. But perhaps Scott had simply found out an important fact: For the past 20 years, Missouri courts had ruled that people taken as slaves into free states and territories and then returned to Missouri were no longer slaves. The courts reasoned, "Once free, always free."

Illinois, the site of Fort Armstrong, had outlawed slavery in its Constitution. Fort Snelling in the Minnesota Territory sat on free ground (declared so by Congress in the Missouri Compromise of 1820). Missouri's Supreme Court had already considered a case much like Scott's. An Army officer had taken his slave named Rachel to Fort Snelling and returned her to St. Louis. In 1837, the court freed her. Scott's case seemed open and shut.

Scott needed special permission to pursue his case because normally slaves could not bring suits. But Missouri had passed a law giving slaves a way to sue for freedom.

The Missouri Courts

Scott's case went to trial in June 1847. It ended abruptly with the judge directing the jury to bring back a verdict against Scott. Scott's attorneys had made an error and failed to prove one

Dred Scott (c. 1795–1858), a slave, sued for his freedom in 1846. His case was finally decided by the U.S. Supreme Court in 1857.

part of the case: that Emerson was holding Scott as a slave. After the verdict, the judge granted Scott's lawyers' request for a new trial to correct their error. At the second trial, the jury ruled in the Scotts' favor. Dred, Harriet, Eliza, and Lizzy were officially free.

As soon as the jury took away her property, Irene Emerson asked for a third trial. The judge turned her down. Then her lawyers appealed to the Missouri Supreme Court. In doing so, they ended the Scotts' brief freedom. Until the case was settled, the family would be treated as slaves.

In the appeal, Emerson's lawyers said that the judge at the second trial had misinformed the jury about a matter of law when he told them that residence in a free area entitled a slave to freedom. In the past, they admitted, Missouri courts had upheld this idea. But it was "based upon false legal principles." It should now be rejected.

No state is forced to accept the laws of other states or territories, the lawyers argued. A state should only do so if those laws supported its own interests. Freeing slaves was not in Missouri's interests. In fact, the free blacks living in the state posed a threat. They would "dissatisfy and corrupt those of their own race and color remaining in a state of servitude."

Scott's lawyers responded that his freedom was a well-established matter of law. In more than 12 cases, the state Supreme Court had held that slaves taken into free territory and returned to Missouri were free. One case, Rachel's, was almost exactly like Scott's. The court should uphold these decisions, they said, because the law depended on consistent rulings.

In 1852, the three-judge Missouri Supreme Court announced its decision. Justice William Scott, with Justice John Ryland concurring, found for the appellant, Irene Emerson. According to Justice Scott, Dred Scott had been free at Fort Snelling, but he gave up any claims to freedom when he returned to Missouri. In spite of precedent, once free did not have to mean always free. The justice wrote:

> Every state has the right of determining how far it will respect the laws of the other states. No state is bound to carry into effect enactments conceived in a spirit hostile to that which pervades her own laws. . . . It is a humiliating spectacle to see the courts of a State confiscating the property of her own citizens by the command of a foreign law.

Once, he noted, Missouri had respected the emancipation laws of free states and territories. But "times now are not what they were when former decisions were made," said the justice. He pointed out that Northern abolitionists, often with the support of government, were trying to destroy slavery. The justice no longer saw any reason why Southern states should comply with their enemies' laws.

Chief Justice Hamilton Gamble disagreed. His dissent made three main points:

1. Emancipation was regulated by written laws clearly stating that after fulfilling certain requirements, slaves had the right to their freedom.

2. By residing in Illinois and at Fort Snelling, Dred Scott fulfilled the necessary requirements, and therefore became free.

3. Once obtained, freedom cannot be taken away.

Gamble argued that these matters of law should not be overturned because of the wrongful actions of abolitionists. Their actions had no bearing on the case. "Times may have changed," said Gamble, "public feeling may have changed, but principles have not and do not change, and in my judgment there can be no safe basis for judicial decisions, but in those principles which are immutable."

Making a Federal Case

People who lose state high-court decisions can, in certain cases, appeal them to the U.S. Supreme Court. Dred Scott could have done that. But a few years before, the court on technical grounds had refused jurisdiction on a case challenging "once free, always free." Scott's legal advisors feared the court would also refuse to hear his case.

To obtain redress from the federal courts, Scott needed a new case, a case with clear federal jurisdiction. By chance, Irene Emerson had moved to Massachusetts where she met and married Calvin Chaffee, an abolitionist doctor. Irene Emerson Chaffee was now a citizen of Massachusetts. Under the Constitution, a citizen of a different state, such as Missouri, could sue her in federal court. Slaves were not citizens, but Scott claimed he wasn't a slave.

In November 1853, a year and a half after the Missouri Supreme Court's decision, Scott's lawyers filed a suit on his behalf in federal court. They charged Scott's owners with civil assault and asked for $9,000 damages. This time, though, Scott did not sue Irene Emerson Chaffee. He sued her brother, John Sanford.

John Sanford and his father had handled Irene's business affairs after her first husband's death. Sanford, too, had moved out of state to New York, where he was active in the pro-slavery wing of the Democratic Party. In suing Sanford, Scott's lawyers made a mistake. Sanford did not legally own the Scotts. Sanford could easily have objected citing this reason and stopped the case.

Instead, Sanford's attorneys objected on other grounds. They claimed that since Scott was black and black people were not citizens, the federal court had no jurisdiction. Attorney Roswell Field replied that free black people could be citizens under certain conditions. On this matter of law, Judge Robert Wells ruled that anyone born in the United States and capable of owning property was a citizen having the right to sue. If Scott was free, he could own property. A trial would have to be held to determine whether Scott was free.

At the trial on Monday, May 15, 1854, the two sides did not dispute the facts. No witnesses were called. Both sides agreed that the Scotts had traveled to free areas and that John Sanford, claiming to be their current owner, continued to treat the family as slaves. Scott's lawyers argued that given these facts, the law said the Scotts were free. Sanford's attorneys claimed the contrary.

Judge Robert W. Wells' sympathies favored the Scotts, but his understanding of federal law supported Sanford. He told the jury that as a matter of law, taking a slave into a free area only suspended slavery. Returning to a slave state renewed the owner's property rights. Since Northern laws freeing slaves deprived owners of their property rights, slave states could ignore them. Given these instructions, the jury found for the defendant. Claiming that the judge misinformed the jury, Scott's lawyers appealed to the Supreme Court.

So far Dred Scott's case had not drawn much attention. Few knew about his eight-year struggle for freedom, even in St. Louis. Only one local paper mentioned the federal verdict. Soon, though, Dred Scott would be famous.

The Heightening Conflict

By the early 1850s, the nation was mired in conflicts that led to the Civil War. One major conflict was over whether Congress could tell new states joining the Union whether they could practice slavery. For years, as new states organized in the territories, Congress had tried to keep a balance between the number of slave and free states. In 1820, as part of the Missouri Compromise, Congress agreed that no new slave states would be formed out of any part of the Louisiana Purchase north of Missouri's southern border. This compromise kept Congress quiet on the slavery question for 30 years.

Just two weeks after Judge Wells' decision, President Franklin Pierce signed the Kansas-Nebraska Act. With this new law, Congress reversed the Missouri Compromise and said people in the newly forming states could decide for themselves whether they wanted slavery. Advocates on both sides rushed to the territories to sway these elections.

The Supreme Court

By the end of 1854, the Supreme Court agreed to review Scott's case. Due to a clerical error that was never corrected, the case was known as *Dred Scott v. Sandford*, not Sanford. As the case moved forward on the court's docket, Scott's friends published an appeal for funds and legal assistance. A prominent Maryland lawyer, Montgomery Blair, agreed to argue the case at no charge. An anti-slavery paper volunteered to cover his expenses.

The Supreme Court did not hear Scott's case until February 1856. At the hearing, Blair repeated Scott's case for freedom, and the other side stressed Scott's voluntary return to slave territory. Sanford's lawyers also introduced a new argument. They claimed Scott was not on free soil when he was at Fort Snelling. The fort was not a free area because Congress had no right to forbid slavery in the territories.

The court retired to consider the case. But after several days of intense debate, the justices could

An advocate of states rights and a proponent of slavery, Roger Taney (1777–1864) was chief justice for more than 30 years. His decision in the *Dred Scott* case drew great controversy.

not reach a majority opinion. Questions about the decision and its potential impact began to seep into the papers. Then in mid-May, Chief Justice Roger Taney announced that the court wanted to rehear the case. He said that the attorneys should pay special attention to two points: Did federal courts have jurisdiction? Was Scott a citizen?

Two weeks after Taney's announcement, pro-slavery raiders slaughtered "free state" homesteaders in Lawrence, Kansas. The next day, a pro-slavery Congressman beat up an abolitionist Senator on the Senate floor. Two days later, a "free state" raid left five pro-slavery settlers dead. That fall's presidential election—at heart a contest between the pro-slavery Democrats and the abolitionist Republicans—continued to inflame tempers. The Democrats' narrow victory settled nothing.

By December 15, when the Supreme Court began its second round, interest in Scott's case had

grown intense. Spectators packed the court's chambers. Some newspapers carried the oral arguments word for word. As the justices debated in private through January and February, so did the public and Congress. In his inaugural address, President James Buchanan urged Americans to honor the court's decision "whatever this may be."

Two days later, on March 6, 1857, the Supreme Court announced its decision. By a vote of 7 to 2, the court ruled in favor of Sanford. All nine justices wrote separate opinions. But Chief Justice Taney, a strong believer in slavery, seemed to speak for a majority of the justices, and the views he expressed were extreme.

Taney's Decision

Taney's decision consisted of two main points. First, the court did not have jurisdiction to hear the case. Article III of the Constitution gave the court authority to hear cases "between Citizens of different States." Taney ruled, however, that people of African ancestry—whether free or slave—were not U.S. citizens and therefore had no right to sue in federal court.

Since he ruled that the court did not have jurisdiction to hear the case, his decision should have stopped there. But Taney went on to decide the merits of the case.

His second point was that Scott was never a free man. When Scott went to Fort Snelling in the Minnesota Territory, he had not gone into free territory. Congress had said this was free territory in the Missouri Compromise. But Taney ruled that Congress had overstepped its powers, and therefore the Missouri Compromise was unconstitutional. Scott had, however, entered Illinois, a free state. But Taney argued that entering the state did not make Scott a free man unless Missouri law said that it did. Taney pointed out that the Missouri Supreme Court had already ruled against Scott on this matter.

     Landmarks: Historic U.S. Supreme Court Decisions

Aftermath

In one decision, Taney tried to settle all the questions of slavery in favor of the South. But the decision just worsened the situation and left no room for compromise. When Republican Abraham Lincoln won the presidency in 1860, most Southern states tried to secede from the Union, and soon the Civil War began.

As for Dred Scott and his family, they were freed shortly after the Supreme Court's decision. Dr. Chaffee had not known that his wife owned slaves until a month before the decision. He had the Scotts freed. Outwardly, the Scotts' lives continued much the same. Harriet worked as a washerwoman; Dred as a porter. Now famous, Dred got offers from promoters to tour as an exhibition. Harriet would have none of it. Dred Scott died in St. Louis of tuberculosis in September 1858. Harriet died soon after. Only Lizzy, their youngest child, survived the Civil War.

For Discussion

1. It took 11 years from the time Dred Scott sued until the decision of the U.S. Supreme Court. Describe the case's path through the courts.

2. What was Dred Scott's claim based on? How did the Missouri Supreme Court ultimately rule on this claim? Do you think its decision was justified under Missouri law? Explain.

3. What two important and controversial points did Chief Justice Roger Taney make in his *Dred Scott* decision?

4. The court's opinion in *Dred Scott* is considered one of the worst in the court's history. Why do you think it is? How might Taney have written an opinion ruling in favor of Sanford without creating such a furor?

Amending the Constitution

Since the *Dred Scott* decision interpreted the meaning of the Constitution, Congress could not simply pass a law to overturn the decision. The Supreme Court has the final word on the meaning of the Constitution. There are just two ways of overruling a Supreme Court decision on the meaning of the Constitution:

1. The Supreme Court in a subsequent decision may overrule it.

2. The Constitution may be amended. This may be done in two ways. One is a constitutional convention. (This method has never been used.) The other method is for both houses of Congress to approve by a two-thirds majority an amendment to the Constitution, which must be ratified by three-fourths of the state legislatures.

Imagine that you are members of a congressional subcommittee following the Civil War. Your task is to write a proposed amendment to the U.S. Constitution that will, in effect, overrule the *Dred Scott* decision.

As a group, do the following:

1. Review the section of the article titled "Taney's Decision." Write down what parts of the decision you want your amendment to overturn.

2. Draft an amendment that will overturn these parts of the decision. Your amendment should not say, "The *Dred Scott* decision is overruled." You must craft an amendment creating clear rules that will forever prevent a ruling similar to *Dred Scott*.

3. Be prepared to present your amendment to the class and explain how it overrules the *Dred Scott* decision.

The Separate but Equal Doctrine

The Supreme Court's decision in *Plessy* gave legal support to segregation in all areas—schools, parks, hotels, restaurants, theaters, and even bus waiting rooms.

As originally written, the U.S. Constitution did little to protect the rights of African Americans. It did not abolish slavery. It offered little protection from racial discrimination. Following the Civil War, however, three amendments were added to the Constitution. The 13th Amendment abolished slavery and "involuntary servitude" (except for convicted prisoners). The 14th Amendment granted citizenship to everyone born in the United States. It also banned states from limiting citizens' rights, depriving anyone of due process of law, or denying "any person . . . the equal protection of the laws." The 15th Amendment prohibited states from denying citizens the right to vote because of "race, color, or previous condition of servitude." These amendments offered promises that African Americans would finally achieve equal treatment under the law.

The slaves were freed, and for a few years blacks exercised previously unknown freedoms during Reconstruction when federal troops occupied the defeated South. But the rights of African Americans declined dramatically after federal troops withdrew in 1877. With local white rule restored, Southern blacks lived under a constant threat of violence. Those seeking to vote were frequently intimidated. Southern states started adopting Jim Crow laws, which established different rules for black and white people. These laws ordered strict racial segregation in all public areas, including hospitals, restaurants, hotels, trains and buses, playgrounds, and even cemeteries. Signs marked "white"and "colored" dominated the South, ensuring that African Americans would be treated as second-class citizens.

The *Plessy* Case

In 1892, a group of black professionals in New Orleans decided to challenge a Louisiana Jim Crow law, the Separate Car Act. This law required that passenger trains provide separate but equal compartments "for the white, and colored races." Anyone sitting in the wrong compartment could be fined $25 or spend 20 days in jail.

The group called itself the Citizens Committee to Test the Constitutionality of the Separate Car Law. It was supported by the East Louisiana Railroad Company, which objected to the expense of providing separate railroad cars for the two races.

The citizens committee enlisted Homer Plessy, a 29-year-old shoemaker, to take part in the test case. Plessy was only one-eighth black. (One of his eight great-grandparents was black.) He appeared to be white, but under Louisiana law, he was black.

Plessy bought a first-class ticket from New Orleans to Covington, Louisiana. Dressed in a suit like the other first-class passengers, he boarded without incident. As planned, when the conductor collected his ticket, Plessy informed him that according to state law, he was a colored man. The conductor told him that he would have to sit in the car reserved for blacks. Plessy refused to move. As arranged in advance, the conductor called a private detective, who took Plessy into custody. Turned over to the police, Plessy was charged with violating the Separate Car Law.

The case was heard in Louisiana criminal court before Judge John Howard Ferguson. This judge had previously heard another test case brought by the citizens committee. He had ruled unconstitutional a Louisiana law mandating separate railroad cars on interstate trains. The law in Plessy's case applied only to trains running within the state. Ferguson ruled that this law was constitutional because he believed a state had a right to enforce segregation within its own borders. Plessy appealed this ruling to the Louisiana Supreme Court. (The case was named *Plessy v. Ferguson* because Plessy was challenging the decision of Judge Ferguson.) When the Louisiana Supreme Court affirmed the ruling, Plessy appealed to the U.S. Supreme Court.

Justice John Marshall Harlan (1833–1911) wrote a stirring dissent in *Plessy v. Ferguson*.

The Supreme Court Decision

Plessy argued that Louisiana's Jim Crow law violated both the 13th and 14th amendments. By a 7–1 vote in *Plessy v. Ferguson*, the court rejected Plessy's arguments.

Writing for the majority, Justice Henry Brown held that this law had nothing to do with slavery and therefore it did not violate the 13th Amendment. He also ruled that the 14th Amendment only called for *legal* equality. It was not intended to enforce the *social* equality of the races in America. He maintained that laws requiring the separation of the races implied no inferiority of either race. They were, he argued, merely passed to protect the common good, not to annoy or oppress anyone. Brown stated that if black people regarded such laws as a badge of inferiority, that was merely their interpretation. He ruled that segregated facilities in public transportation and other areas of life, including education, were constitutionally permissible, as long such facilities were equal. This case created the "separate but equal" doctrine.

The sole dissenter, Justice John Harlan, blasted the decision, calling it one of the worst decisions the court had ever made. Harlan predicted that the judgment of the court in *Plessy* "will, in time, prove to be quite as pernicious as the decision made by this tribunal in the Dred Scott Case."

The *Dred Scott* case was a Supreme Court decision made before the Civil War. It ruled that blacks could never be citizens and that Congress had no power to outlaw slavery in American territories. The amendments after the Civil War overruled the *Dred Scott* decision. It would take another six decades before *Plessy* was overruled by the Supreme Court in *Brown v. Board of Education*.

In the meantime, the decision in *Plessy v. Ferguson* gave segregation a solid legal foundation. Jim Crow laws and segregation grew throughout the South. No major challenges were mounted against them for many years.

For Discussion

1. What constitutional amendments were enacted following the Civil War? What was their purpose?

2. What were Jim Crow laws? What was their purpose?

3. What was the Separate Car Law? Who supported Plessy's making his test case challenging the Separate Car Law? Why do you think they chose Plessy?

4. Judge Ferguson, the trial judge, had decided a similar case before Plessy's. What was the case? How did he decide? How did the judge justify his different opinions in the two cases?

5. Plessy charged that the Separate Car Law violated the 13th and 14th amendments. How did the Supreme Court's opinion rule on these claims? Do you think the law violated the two amendments? Explain.

6. History has validated Justice Harlan's prediction that the *Plessy* decision was as pernicious as the *Dred Scott* decision. Which do you think was more pernicious? Why?

A Dissent to *Plessy*

Dissenting opinions can be important in the development of law. They are written to galvanize the opinion of the public and of legal scholars in the hope that the current court opinion will someday be overruled. Dissents provide the thinking and reasoning that future courts might use to overrule a decision.

In *Plessy v. Ferguson*, Justice Harlan was the only dissenter. He believed that Jim Crow laws violated both the 13th and 14th amendments. Imagine that you are part of Justice Harlan's chambers. Write Harlan's dissent in *Plessy v. Ferguson*. It should consist of three paragraphs:

Paragraph 1. Explain why Jim Crow laws violate the 13th Amendment.

Paragraph 2. Explain why Jim Crow laws violate the 14th Amendment.

Paragraph 3. Explain why the opinion of the court in *Plessy* is wrong and will harm American society.

Select a member of your group to role play Justice Harlan. The other members of your group role play Justice Harlan's law clerks. Justice Harlan should next:

1. Lead a discussion to develop reasons for each paragraph. In your discussion refer to the amendments written below. The law clerks should take notes on the discussion.

2. Assign law clerks to write the first two paragraphs.

3. Write the third paragraph.

4. Lead a read-through and editing of the completed drafts.

5. Be prepared to read the dissent to the class.

13th Amendment. Neither slavery nor involuntary servitude, except as a punishment for crime . . . , shall exist within the United States . . . .

14th Amendment. All persons born or naturalized in the United States . . . are citizens of the United States and of the State wherein they reside. No State shall make or enforce any law which shall abridge the privileges or immunities of citizens of the United States; nor shall any State . . . deny to any person within its jurisdiction the equal protection of the laws.

Schenck v. U.S. (1919)

Free Speech in Wartime

An anti-war rally in 1914. Many Americans initially opposed the United States entering the Great War. But by the time the United States declared war in 1917, most supported the war.

On April 6, 1917, the United States entered World War I by declaring war on Germany. A few weeks later Congress passed a law that ordered the drafting of young men into the armed forces. Eventually more than a million American soldiers went to Europe to fight in the "Great War." By the time the war ended on November 11, 1918, more than 50,000 Americans had died in combat.

At home most people supported President Woodrow Wilson and the war effort. "The world must be made safe for democracy," Wilson said. Even so, a small number of American pacifists and political radicals spoke out against U.S. participation in the war. The dissenters against the war presented a dilemma for Americans: Just how much free speech should a democracy allow during wartime?

The Espionage Acts

Two months after declaring war, Congress passed the Espionage Act of 1917. Designed mainly to prevent sabotage and spying, the Espionage Act also prohibited any "attempt to cause insubordination, disloyalty, mutiny, or refusal of duty, in the military or naval forces of the United States."

The next year Congress enacted an amendment to the Espionage Act, making it a crime to "willfully obstruct or attempt to obstruct the recruiting or enlistment service of the United States." The amendment also made it illegal to "willfully utter, print, write, or publish any disloyal, profane, scurrilous [insulting], or abusive language about the form of government of the United States, or the Constitution of the United States, or the . . . flag of the United States."

The Espionage Acts of 1917 and 1918 carried penalties of up to $10,000, 20 years in prison, or both. About 2,000 persons were arrested and prosecuted under these laws.

The *Schenck* Case

One of those arrested was Charles T. Schenck, general secretary for the American Socialist Party. During his trial, Schenck admitted printing about 15,000 anti-draft leaflets for distribution to men who had just received their draft notices. Some of the leaflets were mailed directly to drafted men.

After quoting the 13th Amendment (which prohibits slavery), the leaflet stated that a man drafted into the Army was little more than a prison convict. According to the writers of the leaflet, the draft was a monstrous wrong created to keep the war going so businessmen could make more money from it. Under a section titled "Assert Your Rights," the leaflet called upon drafted men to recognize "your right to assert your opposition to the draft."

Schenck and several other Socialist Party members were convicted of violating the parts of the Espionage Acts that prohibited interfering with the draft. Schenck appealed his conviction to the U.S. Supreme Court. He argued that everything he said, wrote, and did was protected by the First Amendment. Among other things, the First Amendment states that "Congress shall make no law . . . abridging the freedom of speech, or of the press."

The *Schenck* case finally reached the Supreme Court two months after the war ended. On March 3, 1919, the court unanimously upheld Schenck's conviction. Justice Oliver Wendell Holmes wrote the decision.

Justice Holmes first rejected Schenck's argument that no evidence proved that the leaflets actually persuaded young men to violate the draft law. Holmes wrote that the *intention* of Schenck and his fellow defendants to obstruct the draft was clear enough to justify their conviction.

But what about the First Amendment? Did Congress itself act illegally by passing laws blocking Schenck's freedom of speech?

Justice Holmes admitted that during peacetime, the leaflet distributed by Schenck and the other Socialists would have been protected by the First Amendment. "But," Justice Holmes went on, "the character of every act depends upon the circumstances in which it is done." The *circumstances* in this case involved not peacetime but wartime.

Justice Holmes next held that freedom of speech may be limited in certain circumstances. "The most stringent protection of free speech would not protect a man in falsely shouting fire in a theatre, and causing a panic," he wrote.

When is the government justified in punishing people for what they say or write? "The question in every case," Holmes answered, "is whether the words are used in such circumstances and are of such a nature as to create a clear and present danger."

In the view of Justice Holmes and the other members of the Supreme Court, wartime was one of those circumstances when certain spoken and written words are too dangerous to allow. "When a nation is at war," Holmes explained, "many things that might be said in time of peace are such a hindrance to its effort that their utterance will not be endured so long as men fight."

Justice Holmes concluded his written opinion by saying that any leaflet that encouraged men "to assert your opposition to the draft" was "a clear and present danger" when the United States was at war. Under these circumstances, the Supreme Court ruled that Schenck and the other defendants had been properly convicted.

The *Abrams* Case

Eight months after deciding the *Schenck* case, the Supreme Court handed down another opinion on free speech during wartime. But this time, the Supreme Court was not unanimous.

Jacob Abrams and four other defendants in this case were immigrants from Russia. They described themselves as "rebels," "revolutionaries," and "anarchists." The group was accused of printing and distributing leaflets that insulted the United States and interfered with the nation's war effort against Germany. The defendants were charged under provisions of the Espionage Acts of 1917 and 1918.

Most of the leaflets in question had been thrown out of a window of a building in New York City on August 22, 1918. This incident took place within a few months of the Russian Communist Revolution of 1917. Soon after this revolution, the new Soviet government ended Russian participation in the war against Germany. The United States and the other Allies deeply opposed the USSR's withdrawal from the war. In response, some of the Allied powers, including the United States, sent troops into parts of the USSR. The five Russian immigrants printed and distributed their leaflet to protest this intervention.

One article in the leaflet denounced President Wilson as a hypocrite and a coward for sending American troops into the USSR. The article appealed for American workers to unite and revolt against the government.

A second article referred to "his Majesty, Mr. Wilson, and the rest of the gang; dogs of all colors!" This article also addressed Russian immigrants working in U.S. ammunition factories: "you are producing bullets, bayonets, cannons, to murder not only the Germans, but also your dearest, best, who are in Russia and are fighting for freedom." The article called for a general strike in the United States "to create so great a disturbance . . . America shall be compelled to keep their armies at home, and not be able to spare any for Russia."

Oliver Wendell Holmes Jr. (1841–1935) served on the Supreme Court for 30 years. Known as a legal scholar, he wrote many often-quoted decisions.

Were the words in this leaflet "a clear and present danger" to the United States, which at the time was still at war in Europe? Seven of the nine Supreme Court justices thought so. (*Abrams v. U.S.*, 1919)

The majority concluded that even if the authors of the leaflet were mainly concerned with the cause of the Russian Revolution, their plan of action included undermining the U.S. war effort. Appealing to workers to stop making ammunition and calling for a general strike during wartime was as much a threat to the country as interfering with the military draft.

Two justices, Louis D. Brandeis and Oliver Wendell Holmes, dissented. They argued that the circumstances in this case did not amount to "a clear and present danger." Justice Holmes, who only a few months earlier had upheld the conviction of Schenck, wrote the dissenting opinion.

Justice Holmes argued that "it is only the present danger of immediate evil or an intent to bring it about" that justifies limiting free speech. Holmes could find no "immediate evil" in what he called "a silly leaflet by an unknown man." He also failed to see any intention on the part of the defendants to hinder America's war against Germany. He wrote that the only purpose of the leaflet was "to help Russia and stop American intervention there."

Justice Holmes also contended that "a clear and present danger" must be a real and immediate threat. He further declared that in a democracy the way to find the truth is "by free trade in ideas—that the best test of truth is the power of the thought to get itself accepted in the competition of the market."

In the *Schenck* case, Justice Holmes recognized that in some circumstances, the government may limit what people say and write. In the *Abrams* case, Holmes warned against excessive attempts by the government to stifle free speech, even in wartime:

> I think that we should be eternally vigilant against attempts to check the opinions that we loathe . . . unless they so imminently threaten immediate interference with the lawful and pressing purposes of the law that an immediate check is required to save the country.

This language would set the tone for debate in free expression cases throughout the 20th century.

For Discussion

1. What were the *Schenck* and *Abrams* cases about? How did Justice Holmes think each case should be decided? What difference in the *circumstances* of the two cases might have caused Justice Holmes to believe they should have been decided differently?

2. Do you think the provisions of the Espionage Acts quoted in the article were necessary during World War I? Why or why not? Are they needed today? Explain.

3. What circumstances, if any, in peacetime might justify the government in placing limits on freedom of press or speech? Why?

When Is Speech a "Clear and Present Danger"?

In addition to *Schenck* and *Abrams*, the Supreme Court decided other similar World War I free-speech cases. In this activity, the class will debate these cases.

Your teacher has assigned your group one of the cases below and a side to take on the case's question—either "pro" or "con." In your group, prepare arguments for your side. Review both the *Schenck* and *Abrams* cases presented in this article.

Pro groups should base their arguments on the *Schenck* case.

Con groups should base their arguments on the dissent in the *Abrams* case.

If your group is involved in Cases A and B, review in your U.S. history textbook what most Americans thought about U.S. participation in World War I.

If your group is involved in Case C, read your U.S. history textbook about the "Red Scare" following the war.

Be prepared to present your arguments to the class.

Free Speech Cases

Case A: *Debs v. U.S.* (1919)

Eugene V. Debs, a leader of the American Socialist Party, addressed an anti-war rally in 1918. At this rally, Debs praised other Socialist leaders who had previously been arrested for opposing the draft law. Debs told his audience (which included draft-age men): "You have your lives to lose . . . . You need to know that you are fit for something better than slavery and cannon fodder." Debs was arrested and tried for violating the 1918 Amendment to the Espionage Act. This law prohibited any speech that interfered with the drafting of men into the armed forces.

Debate Question: Was Eugene V. Debs' speech at the anti-war rally a "clear and present danger" to the national security of the United States?

37

Case B: *Frohwerk v. U.S.* (1919)

Jacob Frohwerk published a pro-German newspaper in Missouri. Shortly after the United States entered World War I, Frohwerk printed a series of 12 articles opposing this action. He was arrested and put on trial for violating the Espionage Act of 1917.

Debate Question: Were Jacob Frohwerk's 12 articles a "clear and present danger" to the national security of the United States?

Case C: *Gitlow v. New York* (1925)

Benjamin Gitlow was a leader of the American Communist Party. After World War I, Gitlow published and distributed 16,000 copies of a Communist Party document called the "Left Wing Manifesto." This document argued for a Communist revolution in the United States and urged labor strikes and "class action . . . having as its objective the conquest of the power of the state." Gitlow was arrested by New York authorities for violating that state's Criminal Anarchy Act. This law made it a felony to advocate overthrowing established government by force or violence.

Debate Question: Was Benjamin Gitlow's "Left Wing Manifesto" a "clear and present danger" to the national security of the United States?

Debriefing Questions

1. What were the most important differences in the circumstances of these three cases?

2. Try to write a specific definition of "a clear and present danger." Do you think this is an easy or a difficult task? Why?

A watercolor painting of Baltimore's harbor shows ships and wharves with the city in the background.

In 1815, John Barron, a successful businessman, owned a wharf located at the deepest part of Baltimore's harbor. That year, several city street-improvement projects diverted streams, which caused soil to build up in front of Barron's wharf. By 1822, no ships could tie up at the wharf, and John Barron was out of business.

Barron went to a state court and sued the city of Baltimore for destroying his wharf business. According to the Fifth Amendment of the U.S. Constitution, Barron argued, private property could not be taken or reduced in value for public use without "just compensation." The case finally ended up before the U.S. Supreme Court. Writing for a unanimous Supreme Court, Chief Justice John Marshall dismissed Barron's lawsuit. The court ruled that the Fifth Amendment, as well as the other amendments of the Bill of Rights, applied only to the national government and not to the states (*Barron v. Baltimore*, 1833).

The *Barron* decision established the principle that the rights listed in the original Bill of Rights did not control state laws or actions. A state could abolish freedom of speech, establish a tax-supported church, or do away with jury trials in state courts without violating the Bill of Rights.

The Due Process Clause

In the first Congress in 1789, Congressman James Madison had submitted proposed constitutional amendments for the Bill of Rights. One of Madison's proposed amendments would have prohibited states from violating the rights of conscience, freedom of the press, and trial by jury in criminal cases. The House passed Madison's proposed amendment. But the Senate rejected it because states already had their own bills of rights. The first 10 amendments thus limited only the national government.

When members of Congress debated the 14th Amendment after the Civil War, they hardly discussed whether the amendment made the entire Bill of Rights apply to the states. A key provision of the amendment is its due process clause: ". . . nor shall any State deprive any person of life, liberty, or property, without due process of law . . . ." Did this due process clause apply all the guarantees in the Bill of Rights to the states? Or, did it merely refer to those rights related to a fair trial like the identically worded due process provision in the Fifth Amendment? Raoul Berger (1901–2000), a scholar who wrote extensively on the 14th Amendment, argued that the elusive due process clause was simply intended to protect the civil rights of the ex-slaves in the South following the Civil War.

When the Supreme Court interpreted the 14th Amendment for the first time in 1873, the justices avoided ruling on the meaning of the due process clause (*Slaughterhouse Cases*, 1873). The Supreme Court did eventually begin to rule on its meaning. In 1897, the justices unanimously held that the due process clause required state and local governments to give "just compensation" for taking private property for public purposes. Still, this decision (which would have pleased John Barron) did not connect the due process clause of the 14th Amendment to the Bill of Rights. According to the Supreme Court, "just compensation" was a right within the meaning of the due process clause itself (*Chicago Burlington & Quincy Railroad Co. v. Chicago*, 1897).

The Supreme Court first applied the Bill of Rights to the states in 1925 in the *Gitlow v. New York*. Benjamin Gitlow was a Socialist Party member convicted of writing revolutionary pamphlets in violation of New York's Criminal Anarchy Act. His attorneys argued that the New York law violated Gitlow's First Amendment freedom of speech. They contended that the due process clause of the 14th Amendment protected a citizen's freedom of speech against interference from states as well as the national government. While upholding Gitlow's conviction, the Supreme Court ruled for the first time that the First Amendment freedoms of speech and press "are among the fundamental personal rights and liberties protected by the due process clause of the Fourteenth Amendment from impairment by the States."

The *Gitlow* decision did not say that all the protections of the Bill of Rights applied to the states. But the majority of justices agreed that at least some of these rights limited the powers of state and local governments. Following this landmark decision, the Supreme Court on a case-by-case basis applied most of the guarantees of the Bill of Rights to the states. When the last of these cases was decided in 2001, the Supreme Court had created what amounted to a "second bill of rights" limiting the actions of state governments just as the original Bill of Rights had limited the national government. See the chart on page 41.

Palko v. Connecticut

By 1937, freedom of speech, press, religion, assembly, and petition had all been "incorporated" into the 14th Amendment's due process clause. This meant that these First Amendment freedoms were now also part of the 14th Amendment, which limited state laws and actions. The Supreme Court had yet to explain why some rights from the Bill of Rights had been "incorporated" while others had not.

In *Palko v. Connecticut*, a case involving the Fifth Amendment protection against double jeopardy (being tried twice for the same crime), Justice Benjamin Cardozo explained that only

The 'Second Bill of Rights'

Right	Amendment	Supreme Court Case	Date
Freedom of Speech & Press	First	*Gitlow v. New York*	1925
Defense Counsel in Capital Cases	Sixth	*Powell v. Alabama*	1932
Free Exercise of Religion	First	*Hamilton v. Regents of U.C.*	1934
Freedom of Assembly & Petition	First	*DeJonge v. Oregon*	1937
No Establishment of Religion	First	*Everson v. Board of Ed.*	1947
Public Trial	Sixth	*In re Oliver*	1948
No Unreasonable Searches & Seizures	Fourth	*Wolf v. Colorado*	1949
No Cruel & Unusual Punishments	Eighth	*Robinson v. California*	1962
Defense Counsel for Felonies	Sixth	*Gideon v. Wainwright*	1963
No Self-incrimination	Fifth	*Malloy v. Hogan*	1964
Confrontation of Witnesses	Sixth	*Pointer v. Texas*	1965
Impartial Jury Trial	Sixth	*Parker v. Gladden*	1966
Speedy Trial	Sixth	*Klopfer v. North Carolina*	1967
Compulsion of Witnesses to Testify	Sixth	*Washington v. Texas*	1967
Trial by Jury	Sixth	*Duncan v. Louisiana*	1968
No Double Jeopardy	Fifth	*Benton v. Maryland*	1969
Defense Counsel for Crimes with Jail Terms	Sixth	*Argersinger v. Hamilin*	1972
No Excessive Fines	Eighth	*Cooper Industries v. Simmons*	2001

"fundamental rights" need be "incorporated" into the 14th Amendment. He defined these rights as "of the very essence of a scheme of ordered liberty" and "rooted in the tradition and conscience of our people."

While such rights as freedom of speech were clearly "fundamental," according to Justice Cardozo and the Supreme Court majority, others were not. Thus, the Supreme Court established the principle of "partial incorporation": Only certain "fundamental rights," not the entire Bill of Rights, apply to the states through the due process clause of the 14th Amendment.

Incorporation

By 2001, the Supreme Court had "incorporated" into the 14th Amendment all but four rights named in the Bill of Rights. Those rights still not deemed "fundamental" include the Second Amendment right to bear arms, the Third Amendment protection against quartering troops in private homes, the Fifth Amendment right of grand jury indictment, and the Seventh Amendment right of trial by jury in civil cases. (The Ninth and 10th amendments do not name specific personal rights.)

As a practical matter today, the Bill of Rights protects Americans from both national and state governments. In the view of scholar Richard Cortner, the Supreme Court "has transformed the Due Process Clause of the Fourteenth Amendment into our second bill of rights, a bill of rights more salient [significant] to the liberty of the average American than the original document authored by Madison and ratified by the states in 1791."

For Discussion

1. Why did the Bill of Rights originally not apply to the states?

2. What is the doctrine of incorporation?

3. Do you agree or disagree with Richard Cortner that the "second bill of rights" is more significant to average Americans than James Madison's original document? Why?

4. Another scholar, Raoul Berger, criticizes the Supreme Court for creating a "second bill of rights." "At stake is the integrity of the Constitution, the right of the people to govern themselves," he writes. "Whence does the Court derive authority to bring the Constitution in tune with its own predilections [opinions]?" Do you agree or disagree with Berger's view? Explain why.

5. Which four protections or rights so far have not been incorporated into the 14th Amendment? Should all the protections listed in the Bill of Rights apply to the states as well as to the national government? Why or why not?

ACTIVITY

Fundamental Rights

Imagine that your group is a committee of the United Nations and has been asked to work on the following hypothetical case:

Every country in the world has agreed to maintain fundamental human rights. Using the U.S. Bill of Rights as a model, a special committee has reported back to the United Nations with a list of 22 rights. Many countries believe this list includes too many rights. The United Nations has now forwarded this list to your group with instructions to choose the seven most fundamental of these 22 rights. Because the United Nations may ultimately decide to include more or fewer than seven rights, you are also supposed to rank the rights in order of importance from 1 to 22 (1 is the most important; 22 the least important). You should also cross out any rights on the list that you think are not fundamental human rights and add any fundamental rights not currently on the list. (To decide what rights are fundamental, it may be helpful for you to refer to Justice Cardozo's definition of fundamental human rights in the article.)

Be prepared to explain your group's conclusions to the rest of the class.

List of 22 Rights

Protection from Cruel & Unusual Punishments

Freedom from Establishment of Religion

Right to a Public Trial

Protection Against Unreasonable Searches and Seizures

Right to Defense Counsel in Criminal Cases

Protection from Self-Incrimination

Right of Grand Jury Indictment

Free Exercise of Religion

Right to Confront Witnesses at a Trial

Right to an Impartial Jury Trial

Right to a Speedy Trial

Protection Against Quartering Troops in Private Homes

Freedom of Assembly & Petition

Right to Compulsory Process in Obtaining Witnesses

Right to a Trial by Jury in all Major Criminal Cases

Protection Against Double Jeopardy

Right to Bear Arms

Freedom of Speech & Press

Right of Trial by Jury in Civil Cases

Protection from Excessive Bail and Fines

Right to Compensation for Private Property taken by the Government

Right to Privacy

Brown v. Board of Education (1954)

The End of Legal Segregation

Three years after the *Brown* decision, members of the 101st Airborne Division escorted nine African-America students to Little Rock Central High School in Arkansas. The governor had previously sent the National Guard to prevent the students from entering.

Immediately following the Civil War, Reconstruction in the South offered African Americans new freedoms. The Civil War amendments ended slavery, granted them citizenship, promised equal treatment under the law, and guaranteed the right to vote. Blacks voted, won elected office, and served on juries. In 1877, however, federal troops withdrew from the South, returning it to local white rule.

Over the next 20 years, blacks lost almost all they had gained. Worse, denial of their rights and freedoms would be made legal by a series of racist statutes, the Jim Crow laws, mandating the separation of the races.

In 1890, the Louisiana General Assembly passed a law to prevent black and white people from riding together on railroads. *Plessy v. Ferguson*, a case challenging the law, reached the U.S. Supreme Court in 1896. Upholding the law, the court said that public facilities for blacks and whites could be "separate but equal."

Soon Jim Crow laws ordered segregation throughout the South, touching every part of life. In South Carolina, black and white textile workers could not work in the same room or even enter through the same door. Mobile, Alabama, passed a Jim Crow curfew: Blacks could not leave their homes after 10 p.m.

    Landmarks: Historic U.S. Supreme Court Decisions

Signs marked "Whites Only" or "Colored" hung over doors, ticket windows, and drinking fountains. Georgia had black and white parks. Oklahoma had black and white phone booths. Prisons, hospitals and orphanages were segregated as were schools and colleges.

The decision in *Plessy v. Ferguson* gave segregation a solid legal foundation. No major challenge was mounted against it for many years. The National Association for the Advancement of Colored People (NAACP), the leading civil rights organization, concentrated on other battles, such as campaigning against lynching and trying to ensure fair trials for criminal defendants.

In the 1930s, however, the NAACP began challenging legal segregation. Led initially by Charles Houston and later by Thurgood Marshall, NAACP attorneys started the legal battle by focusing on graduate and professional school education. They believed that winning legal battles for integration at this level would be easiest and would create the legal basis for a broader attack on racial segregation. The efforts of the NAACP represent one of the greatest legal strategies in American history. Many of these courageous lawyers risked their personal safety when they traveled through the South, often meeting hostility from police and other whites.

Graduate School Desegregation Cases

Their initial efforts brought significant legal success. Known generally as the "graduate school desegregation cases," these early victories broke down the myth of "separate but equal" facilities for advanced black students. In 1936, a federal appeals court ordered the University of Maryland to admit to its law school a black student it had rejected due to his race. The state had no separate facility for blacks. Two years later, the U.S. Supreme Court ordered the University of Missouri Law School to admit a black student it had excluded. The state had no separate law school for blacks, but had offered to send the student to an out-of-state school for blacks. The court ruled that this offer did not "remove the discrimination," which violated the 14th Amendment.

The Second World War temporarily halted the graduate school cases. But following the war came its two most significant victories. The first involved a black law student, Herman Sweatt, who was denied admission to the University of Texas Law School because of his race. Responding to Sweatt's lawsuit, the state of Texas built a separate law school in Austin for black students. It consisted of three small basement rooms in an office building not far from both the state capitol and the whites-only law school of the University of Texas.

After five years of litigation, Sweatt won his case. In 1950 in *Sweatt v. Painter*, the U.S. Supreme Court unanimously ordered his admission to the University of Texas. It rejected the state's argument that the newly established law school for blacks was even remotely equal to the facilities for white law students.

In the second case, a federal court had ordered the University of Oklahoma to admit a black graduate student. The university had admitted the student, but roped him off from other students, reserving a special section for him in classes, at the library, and in the cafeteria. In 1950 in *McLaurin v. Oklahoma State Regents for Higher Education*, a unanimous Supreme Court ordered the school to end this segregation. The court stated that under the 14th Amendment, the student "must receive the same treatment . . . as students of other races."

Other NAACP Victories

During the 1940s, NAACP lawyers had achieved other significant victories. In *Morgan v. Virginia*, the Supreme Court struck down segregation on interstate transportation because it impeded interstate commerce. In *Smith v. Allwright*, the court ruled that the Southern practice of holding whites-only primary elections violated the 15th Amendment.

Three leading civil rights attorneys posed for a photograph following the Supreme Court's decision in *Brown*. From left to right are George E.C. Hayes, Thurgood Marshall, and James Nabrit. In 1967, Marshall was appointed to the Supreme Court.

In 1948 in *Shelley v. Kraemer*, the court struck down racial restrictive covenants. Common in many parts of the country, these were agreements, often recorded in deeds, that an owner would not sell the land to specified minorities. In this case, despite a covenant against selling to blacks or Asians, the owner sold the property to a black couple. The other property owners sued in state court to prevent the sale. When the case reached the Supreme Court, NAACP attorneys argued that enforcing these covenants violated the 14th Amendment's guarantee of equal protection under the law. The property owners argued that the 14th Amendment only protected against state action and since these private agreements did not involve the state, the 14th Amendment did not apply. The Supreme Court agreed that the agreements by themselves did not involve state action. But the unanimous court pointed out that enforcing them required state action and thus violated the 14th Amendment.

The *Brown* Decision

By the 1950s, the rigid legal doctrine supporting segregation had finally been weakened. Thurgood Marshall was preparing for the final legal assault on school segregation, but he faced major opposition even from many committed to full racial equality. They thought that the time was not ripe for such drastic social and legal change. They feared that the Supreme Court would reject a case seeking total racial integration throughout American public education. Such a defeat, they argued, would result in further frustration and continued racial inequality and lack of opportunity.

Determined to succeed, Marshall pushed ahead. The Supreme Court agreed to hear cases that presented the same issue: Was it legal to mandate separation of the races in public schools?

Two of the cases came from South Carolina and Virginia. Parents had sued to get their children into white schools. In both cases, federal courts had upheld segregation. In a similar case, Delaware's Supreme Court had ordered a district to admit black students to white schools until adequate classrooms could be provided for blacks. The final case was from Topeka, Kansas. The Topeka schools for blacks and whites were equally good, but Oliver Brown wanted his 8-year-old daughter, Linda, to attend a school close to home. State law prevented the white school from accepting Linda because she was black, and the appeals court upheld the law. All the cases had been appealed to the Supreme Court. The court agreed to consider the four cases together.

NAACP lawyers worked furiously to present the best possible case. In 1952, Marshall presented the legal argument to the court. In chambers, the justices were divided. Several justices were concerned about the probable reaction of violence and civil disorder among white Southerners if the court ruled school segregation unconstitutional. Chief Justice Fred Vinson, who had written earlier opinions striking down segregation in universities, appeared reluctant to extend those opinions to the public schools.

Vinson died in the summer of 1953 before a final decision in the case. President Dwight Eisenhower appointed Earl Warren as his replacement. Warren resigned as governor of California to take the position of chief justice.

The court heard a second round of oral arguments on the case. Chief Justice Warren was determined to overturn the "separate but equal" doctrine and equally determined to orchestrate a unanimous decision in a case of such political magnitude. With the assistance of Justice Felix Frankfurter, the new chief justice used his considerable political skills to accomplish this goal.

On May 17, 1954, the Supreme Court announced its dramatic unanimous decision in the landmark case of *Brown v. Board of Education*. Segregation of children in America's public schools, when authorized or required by state law, violated the U.S. Constitution, specifically the 14th Amendment's guarantee of equal protection of the law. Chief Justice Warren's opinion relied on scientific evidence in concluding that segregated schools promoted feelings of inferiority in black children. Because this reduced their motivation to learn, Warren and his fellow justices determined that segregated educational facilities were inherently unequal.

Aftermath

The *Brown* decision was one of the most important in the 20th century. More than any other case, it expanded the legal rights of African Americans. For the first time, many blacks saw that American justice system might actually help them achieve full justice and equality. Robert Williams, a Marine Corps veteran and a civil rights leader, spoke for many:

> On this momentous night of May 17, 1954, I felt that at last the government was willing to assert itself on behalf of first-class citizenship, even for Negroes. I experienced a sense of loyalty that I had never felt before.

For all its historic and constitutional significance in declaring equal educational opportunity, the *Brown* decision was deliberately limited in language and scope. Warren had done this to assure a unanimous decision. The Supreme Court issued no orders to the defendant school boards on when they should end their segregated practices.

The following year, the court decided what is known as *Brown II* on how the *Brown* decision should be implemented. The NAACP argued that schools should be desegregated immediately or on a fixed schedule. The school districts argued that this could not be done and would result in chaos. The Supreme Court in another unanimous decision written by Chief Justice Warren required school boards to "make a prompt and reasonable start" toward compliance. It directed the lower courts to issue orders to schools to admit black children "with all deliberate speed." Such language reflected a concern for the political realities of the time.

Following the Supreme Court's *Brown* decisions, the court continued to strike down legal segregation throughout the 1950s and 1960s. In a series of short opinions, the court outlawed segregation in buses, parks, public golf courses, and other places. In each case, the court cited the *Brown* opinion. In 1967 in *Loving v. Virginia*, the court ruled that states could no longer outlaw people of different races from marrying each other. In that ruling, Chief Justice Warren noted that the Virginia statute, which the court declared invalid, did nothing more than endorse the doctrine of white supremacy. By the end of the 1960s, the court had ended all aspects of legal segregation.

For Discussion

1. What was the Supreme Court's decision in *Plessy v. Ferguson*? What effect did this decision have?

2. Why do you think NAACP attorneys chose graduate schools as their first line of attack on the doctrine of separate but equal?

3. What were restrictive racial covenants? What argument did their defenders use to show that they did not violate the 14th Amendment? How did the Supreme Court rule on these covenants? Do you agree with the court's reasoning? Explain.

4. What was the Supreme Court's decision in *Brown v. Board of Education*? How was this decision extended in later cases?

5. Do you agree with the *Brown II* decision? Explain.

The Meaning of *Brown*

In 2007, the U.S. Supreme Court decided an important school integration case, *Parents Involved in Community Schools v. Seattle School District*. The case consolidated cases from two public school districts—Seattle, Washington, and Louisville, Kentucky. Some parents in both districts objected that their children were assigned to schools based on race.

The school integration plans in the two districts differed. In the Seattle district, high school students could enroll in any of the district's 10 high schools. But when a school was oversubscribed, students were selected based on race to make sure that the school was integrated. The Louisville district plan was based on 25-year-old court-mandated order to desegregate its once legally segregated schools. In 2000, the court lifted the order, but the district decided to keep part of the court's plan to place to prevent the schools from segregating again. The plan requires all non-magnet elementary schools to have a black enrollment of no less than 15 percent and no more than 50 percent.

The U.S. Supreme Court in a 5–4 decision held both plans unconstitutional. The opinion of the court held that public schools could not use race as a basis for assigning students to schools. (The decision was a plurality opinion. Justice Kennedy agreed that the two programs were unconstitutional, but disagreed that race could never be used under any circumstances.)

In this major case, all the written opinions cited the *Brown* decision and claimed to be following *Brown*. (Below are excerpts from the opinion of the court, a concurring opinion, and two dissents.)

Heralded as a great decision, *Brown v. Board of Education* is one of the most important decisions in the history of the Supreme Court. Yet its meaning seems controversial.

• • • • •

Imagine that you are an editorial writer for a major newspaper. You are to write an editorial on the meaning of the *Brown* decision and on which side got the meaning of *Brown* correct in the 2007 decision of *Parents Involved in Community Schools v. Seattle School District*. Support your editorial opinion with material from the article, the 14th Amendment, and the excerpts from the opinions in *Parents Involved in Community Schools v. Seattle School District*.

Chief Justice Roberts (opinion of the court):

What do the racial classifications do in these cases, if not determine admission to a public school on a racial basis? Before *Brown*, schoolchildren were told where they could and could not go to school based on the color of their skin. The school districts in these cases have not carried the heavy burden of demonstrating that we should allow this once again—even for very different reasons. For schools that never segregated on the basis of race, such as Seattle, or that have removed the vestiges of past segregation, such as [Louisville], the way "to achieve a system of determining admission to the public schools on a nonracial basis," [the quote is from *Brown* II] is to stop assigning students on a racial basis. The way to stop discrimination on the basis of race is to stop discriminating on the basis of race.

Justice Thomas (concurring with the opinion of the court):

What was wrong in 1954 cannot be right today. Whatever else the Court's rejection of the segregationists' arguments in *Brown* might have established, it certainly made clear that state and local governments cannot take from the Constitution a right to make decisions on the basis of race . . . . None of the considerations trumpeted by the dissent is relevant to the constitutionality of the school boards' race-based plans because no contextual detail . . . can "provide refuge from the principle that under our Constitution, the government may not make distinctions on the basis of race." [This quote is from his concurring opinion in *Adarand Constructors v. Pena* (1995).]

In place of the color-blind Constitution, the dissent would permit measures to keep the races together and proscribe measures to keep the races apart. Although no such distinction is apparent in the Fourteenth Amendment, the dissent would constitutionalize today's faddish social theories that embrace that distinction. The Constitution is not that malleable. . . . Indeed, if our history has taught us anything, it has taught us to beware of elites bearing racial theories. . . . Can we really be sure that the racial theories that motivated *Dred Scott* and *Plessy* are a relic of the past or that future theories will be nothing but beneficent and progressive? That is a gamble I am unwilling to take, and it is one the Constitution does not allow.

Justice Stevens (dissenting):

There is a cruel irony in The Chief Justice's reliance on our decision in *Brown v. Board of Education.* The first sentence in the concluding paragraph of his opinion states: "Before *Brown,* schoolchildren were told where they could and could not go to school based on the color of their skin." . . . . The Chief Justice fails to note that it was only black schoolchildren who were so ordered; indeed, the history books do not tell stories of white children struggling to attend black schools. In this and other ways, The Chief Justice rewrites the history of one of this Court's most important decisions.

. . .

The Court has changed significantly . . . . It is my firm conviction that no Member of the Court that I joined in 1975 would have agreed with today's decision.

Justice Breyer (dissenting):

For much of this Nation's history, the races remained divided. It was not long ago that people of different races drank from separate fountains, rode on separate buses, and studied in separate schools. In this Court's finest hour, *Brown v. Board of Education* challenged this history and helped to change it. For *Brown* held out a promise. . . . It was the promise of true racial equality—not as a matter of fine words on paper, but as a matter of everyday life in the Nation's cities and schools. . . .

. . . . Today, almost 50 years later, attitudes toward race in this Nation have changed dramatically. Many parents, white and black alike, want their children to attend schools with children of different races. Indeed, the very school districts that once spurned integration now strive for it. The long history of their efforts reveals the complexities and difficulties they have faced. And in light of those challenges, they have asked us not to take from their hands the instruments they have used to rid their schools of racial segregation, instruments that they believe are needed to overcome the problems of cities divided by race and poverty. . . .

The last half-century has witnessed great strides toward racial equality, but we have not yet realized the promise of *Brown.* To invalidate the plans under review is to threaten the promise of *Brown.* The plurality's position . . . is a decision that the Court and the Nation will come to regret.

Mapp v. Ohio (1961)
The Exclusionary Rule

The Fourth Amendment governs how police may conduct searches and obtain evidence. One way of enforcing the Fourth Amendment is the exclusionary rule.

Dollree Mapp lived with her 15-year-old daughter on the top floor of her two-family house in Cleveland, Ohio. She rented the bottom floor to another family. On May 23, 1957, police arrived at her door and demanded entry. Although they gave Mapp no explanation, they were looking for illegal gambling equipment and a suspect in a recent bombing. After phoning her attorney, Mapp refused to let the officers in without a warrant. They left, but kept the house under surveillance. Three hours later, more officers arrived, still without a warrant. They pounded on the door. When Mapp did not come to the door immediately, the police broke into the house.

When they entered, Mapp was coming down the stairs. She demanded to see a warrant. An officer waved a piece of paper at her, but it was not a warrant. She grabbed it and stuffed it down her blouse. The officers forcibly retrieved it and handcuffed her. Then they dragged her upstairs to her bedroom and searched through her belongings and personal papers.

Meanwhile, Mapp's attorney arrived, but the officers would not let him in the house. They continued searching through the rest of the house. After searching everywhere, officers found some obscene materials tucked away in a basement trunk. Mapp was arrested, tried, and convicted of possessing these materials in violation of an Ohio law.

Landmarks: Historic U.S. Supreme Court Decisions

Mapp appealed her conviction to the Ohio Supreme Court. First, she argued that the Ohio obscenity law violated the Constitution. Four of the seven judges on the Ohio Supreme Court agreed. But according to Ohio procedure, six judges had to agree in order to overturn a law as unconstitutional. So the court upheld the law.

Mapp had a second ground for her appeal. She argued that her conviction was based on an illegal search. The state never denied that the search was illegal. Instead, the state argued that the illegal search was irrelevant. Mapp had obscene materials in her basement. She had broken the law and was guilty as charged. Her conviction should not be overturned because of an illegal search. The Ohio Supreme Court agreed, but it did state it would have overturned the conviction if police had removed the evidence from the defendant's body "by the use of brutal or offensive physical force."

Mapp appealed to the U.S. Supreme Court. After oral arguments, all the members of the court in conference agreed that Ohio's obscenity law was unconstitutional. But a majority of the court wanted to decide the case on the issue of the illegal search.

The Law of Search and Seizure

The law of search and seizure comes from the U.S. Constitution's Fourth Amendment. This amendment states:

> The right of the people to be secure in their persons, houses, papers, and effects, against unreasonable searches and seizures, shall not be violated, and no Warrants shall issue, but upon probable cause, supported by Oath or affirmation, and particularly describing the place to be searched, and the persons or things to be seized.

Note that the Fourth Amendment does not ban all searches and seizures by police, government officials, or their agents. It protects against *unreasonable* ones.

With a few exceptions, a search is unreasonable if it is done without "probable cause." Probable cause means that an officer has good reasons for believing that a crime has been committed and the person or place to be searched is related to that crime. Usually, an officer must get a search warrant before conducting a search. A search warrant is a court order signed by a judge authorizing a search. Police can obtain search warrants by showing probable cause exists.

Weeks v. U.S. (1914)

The U.S. Supreme Court had decided two important Fourth Amendment cases before *Mapp*. In 1914, the court decided *Weeks v. U.S.* Police and federal agents in Kansas City, Missouri, had conducted two illegal, warrantless searches of the house of a man named Fremont Weeks. They first entered his house after finding a key under his doormat. When they returned for another search, a boarder let them in. Based on the evidence seized in the illegal searches, Weeks was convicted in federal court of using the mail to transport lottery tickets. Weeks appealed, claiming that the illegal evidence should have been excluded at his trial. A unanimous Supreme Court agreed:

> If letters and private documents can thus be seized and held and used in evidence against a citizen accused of an offense, the protection of the 4th Amendment, declaring his right to be secure against such searches and seizures, is of no value, and, so far as those thus placed are concerned, might as well be stricken from the Constitution.

Thus the Supreme Court created what is known as the exclusionary rule. No evidence obtained in violation of a defendant's Fourth Amendment rights may be presented in court to convict that defendant. Since the Supreme Court had not yet ruled that the Fourth Amendment applied to the states, the exclusionary rule from the *Weeks* case applied only to federal prosecutions.

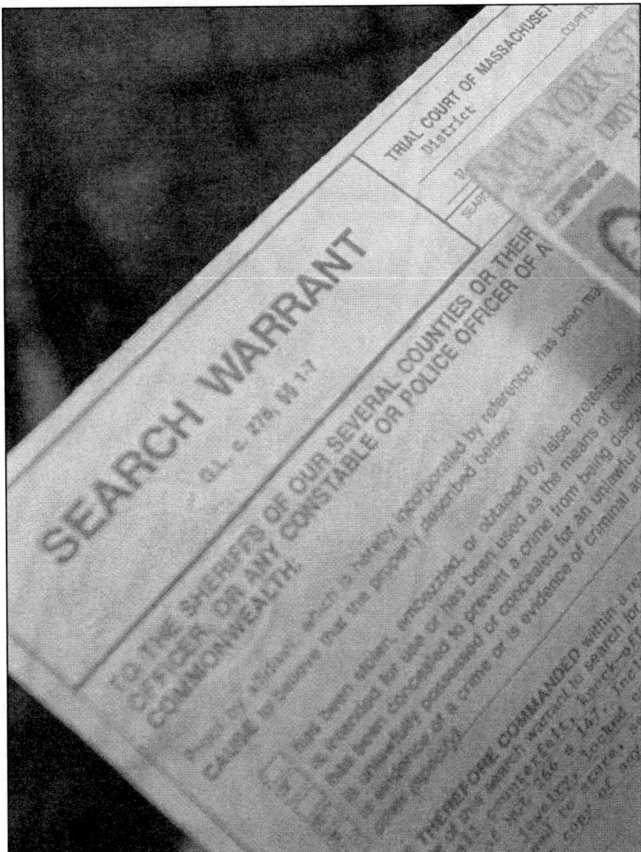

For most searches, police must obtain a search warrant from a judge.

Wolf v. Colorado (1949)

In 1949, all the justices of the Supreme Court in *Wolf v. Colorado* decided that the Fourth Amendment did apply to the states.

> The security of one's privacy against arbitrary intrusion by the police—which is at the core of the Fourth Amendment—is basic to a free society. It is therefore implicit in "the concept of ordered liberty" and as such enforceable against the States through the Due Process Clause [of the 14th Amendment].

But the court was divided on whether the exclusionary rule applied to the states. The 6–3 majority decided that it did not. The court stated that the exclusionary rule was not an essential part of the Fourth Amendment. It noted that every state in the union had constitutions protecting the same rights found in the Fourth Amendment. And so

did all the countries of the English-speaking world. Yet few of these jurisdictions had adopted the exclusionary rule. Of the 47 state courts ruling on the issue, only 17 had adopted the rule. No other jurisdiction in the English-speaking world had adopted it.

The court pointed out that the exclusionary rule only protects those on "whose person or premises something incriminating has been found." If the police make an illegal search and find nothing, the exclusionary rule does not help. A person in that situation must rely on other remedies. For example, a person might file a complaint with the police department. Or a person might file a lawsuit. Or a prosecutor might file a criminal case. These are the normal remedies, and the court found it reasonable for states to rely on these remedies instead of the exclusionary rule.

The dissenters argued that without the exclusionary rule, the Fourth Amendment is a "dead letter." Justice Murphy pointed out that in states with the exclusionary rule, the police were highly trained in the law of search and seizure and instructed to carefully follow it. In states without the rule, little training was given in the law and officers were told that all evidence was admissible. His dissent specifically mentioned three cities where police were given minimal training: New York, Baltimore, and Cleveland (where Dollree Mapp lived).

Mapp v. Ohio (1961)

The *Mapp* case presented an issue that the *Wolf* case had decided just about a decade earlier: Did the Fourth Amendment require that illegally seized evidence be excluded from state trials? This time the Supreme Court by a 5–3 majority concluded that it did, and it overruled the part of the *Wolf* decision that decided otherwise.

Writing for the court majority, Justice Tom Clark said that the Fourth Amendment could not "tolerate denial of its most important constitutional privilege, namely, the exclusion of" illegally seized evidence. "To hold otherwise is to grant

Landmarks: Historic U.S. Supreme Court Decisions

the right but in reality to withhold its privilege and enjoyment."

The court stated that the constitutional right against invasions of privacy by police should not be an empty promise. The court said it could no longer permit this right

> to be revocable at the whim of any police officer who, in the name of law enforcement itself, chooses to suspend its enjoyment. Our decision, founded on reason and truth, gives to the individual no more than that which the Constitution guarantees him, to the police officer no less than that to which honest law enforcement is entitled, and, to the courts, that judicial integrity so necessary in the true administration of justice.

Ruling that "nothing can destroy a government more quickly than its failure to obey its own laws," the court threw out Mapp's conviction and returned the case to a lower court for further proceedings. In doing so, the court extended the exclusionary rule to all criminal trials in the country—both state and federal.

The dissent was divided into two parts. The first part stated that the case should have been decided on the obscenity law. All the justices had agreed that the Ohio obscenity law was unconstitutional. The dissenters believed this issue, which everyone agreed on, was "both simpler and less far reaching." The *Wolf* decision, said the dissenters, simply restated what states had long believed was the rule. By overturning *Wolf*, the court forced changes in the administration of criminal law in many states.

The second part of the dissent argued that the exclusionary rule was not part of the Fourth Amendment. The Supreme Court, as supervisor of the federal courts, could impose the rule on federal courts, but not on state courts.

Justice Potter Stewart joined the first part of the dissent, but refused to participate in the debate over whether the exclusionary rule was mandated by the Fourth Amendment. Hence the vote on the court was 5–3.

The Exclusionary Rule Since *Mapp*

The *Mapp* decision affected police behavior immediately. Police, who had rarely bothered to get warrants, started applying for them. In New York City, for example, police had requested no search warrants in 1960, the year before the *Mapp* decision. The year after *Mapp*, the police requested more than 800 search warrants. The exclusionary rule, with its threat of suppressing illegal evidence, pushed police into seeking warrants.

The *Mapp* decision did not end the debate over the exclusionary rule. Critics of the exclusionary rule believe it hampers the fight against crime. Some argue that too many criminals escape conviction because the rule excludes evidence at trial. Others simply say the rule makes no sense. Justice Benjamin Cardozo reflected this opinion in 1926 when he asked: "Is it right the criminal is to go free because the constable has blundered?"

Supporters of the rule say that it affects few criminal prosecutions, partly because police today do a good job of following proper procedure. In response to critics who claim the procedures themselves hinder law enforcement, supporters point out that these procedures are required by the Constitution. The exclusionary rule simply helps ensure the police follow the Constitution.

For Discussion

1. What is the normal process for obtaining a search warrant? Why do you think they are required by law in most circumstances?

2. What is the exclusionary rule? Why was it established? What justifications are given for it?

3. Do you think it is necessary? Why or why not?

4. Why do you think the court decided *Mapp* on the Fourth Amendment issue instead of on the obscenity issue? Do you think it was proper to do so? Explain.

ACTIVITY

Exceptions to the Exclusionary Rule?

Since the *Mapp* decision, the Supreme Court has heard cases asking the court to carve out exceptions to the exclusionary rule. Imagine that your group is the U.S. Supreme Court and that you are going to decide one of the cases below.

As a group, do the following:

1. Review and discuss the reasons behind the exclusionary rule. The reasons can be found in the first couple of paragraphs under the sections of the article titled *"Weeks v. U.S. (1914)"* and *"Mapp v. Ohio (1961)."*

2. Read and discuss your case.

3. Decide the issue in your case. Think about whether creating an exception to the exclusionary rule in this case would violate the purpose of the rule.

4. Be prepared to report your decision and your reasons to the class.

Cases

A. ***U.S. v. Leon* (1984).** Police put Leon's house under surveillance after an informant told them that Leon was a drug dealer. Based on their observations, police signed an affidavit swearing to what they had observed and used the affidavit to apply for a search warrant. A judge issued a search warrant, and police searched Leon's residence and found large amounts of illegal drugs. Leon was indicted on federal drug charges. His attorneys filed a motion to exclude the evidence from the search because the affidavit applying for the warrant failed to establish probable cause. A judge agreed and ordered the evidence excluded. The prosecution appealed the ruling. The Court of Appeals ruled in favor of Leon. The U.S. Supreme Court granted certiorari. The issue before the court: Should an exception be made to the exclusionary rule when police acting in good faith obtain a warrant that through a judge's error turns out not to be based on probable cause?

B. ***Nix v. Williams* (1984).** Police were searching for the body of a murder victim. They were conducting a large-scale search using 200 volunteers. When they illegally obtained a confession from Williams that indicated where the body was, they called off the search. Williams' confession was excluded at his trial. Williams argued that the evidence of the body's location and condition should not be allowed into evidence because police only found the body due to his illegal confession. The trial court, however, found that the prosecution had shown that "if the search had not been suspended and Williams had not led the police to the victim, her body would have been discovered 'within a short time' in essentially the same condition as it was actually found." The trial court therefore allowed this evidence. Williams was convicted. He appealed, and the case went through several appeals before the U.S. Supreme Court granted certiorari. The issue before the court: Should an exception be made to the exclusionary rule allowing the admission of evidence that would inevitably have been discovered?

C. ***James v. Illinois* (1990).** Eight teenagers returning home from a party were confronted by three other teenagers demanding money. When they refused the demand, one of the three pulled a gun and shot into the group, killing one and seriously injuring another. Eyewitnesses described the shooter as having long straight reddish hair. Following leads, police found James at his mother's beauty salon under a hair dryer. When he got up, his hair was black and curly. Police arrested him, took him to the police station, and questioned him. He admitted to police that he had gone to the beauty shop to change his straight reddish hair. At a pretrial hearing, the judge suppressed James' statements to police because they were obtained following an illegal arrest (the police did not have probable cause to make the arrest). At his trial, James hair was black and curly. Five of the victims identified him as the shooter, but

Landmarks: Historic U.S. Supreme Court Decisions

each also said that the shooter had straight reddish hair. James called a family friend to testify. This witness stated that James had dyed his hair before the night of the murder. Over the defense's objections, the trial judge allowed the prosecution to introduce the illegally obtained statements of James that he had dyed and curled his hair after the murder. James was convicted and appealed. The Illinois Appellate Court agreed that the illegally obtained statements should not have been allowed into evidence, but the Illinois Supreme Court reversed the appellate court. James petitioned for a writ of certiorari to the U.S. Supreme Court. The issue before the court: Should an exception be made to the exclusionary rule? This exception would allow illegally obtained evidence to be introduced to impeach witnesses. The purpose of this rule would be to deter the defense from calling witnesses who will commit perjury.

Gideon v. Wainwright (1963)

The Right to Legal Counsel

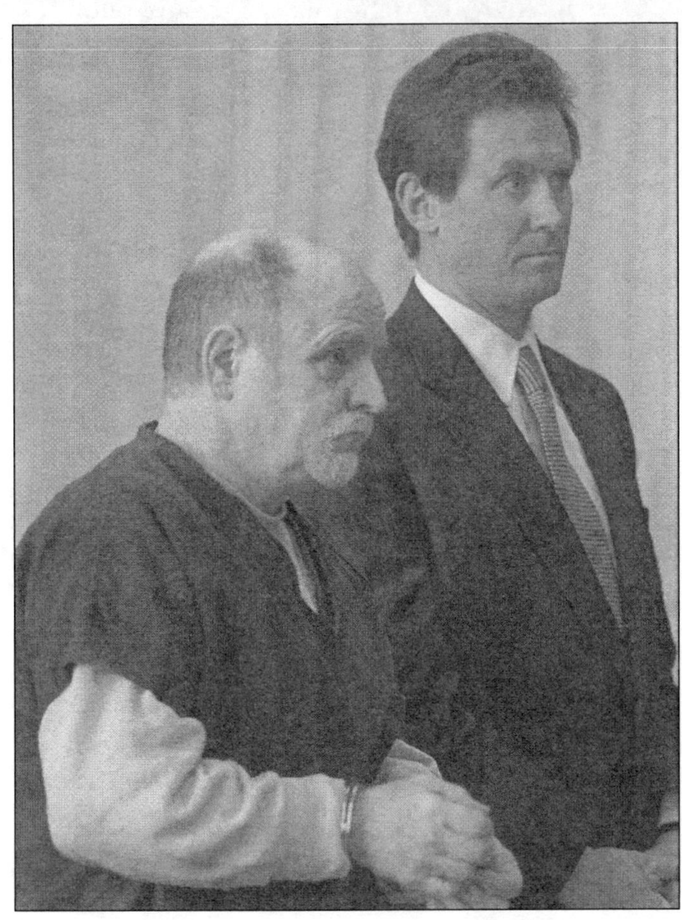

Many criminal defense attorneys today are paid by the government. They usually are either appointed by a judge or members of a public defenders office.

In all criminal prosecutions, the accused shall enjoy the right . . . to have the Assistance of Counsel for his defence.
—Sixth Amendment, U.S. Constitution

In 1942, the Supreme Court ruled that a criminal defendant who could not afford a lawyer did *not* have a constitutional right to have a lawyer appointed to represent him in a state court. Twenty-one years later, faced with a similar set of facts, the court changed its mind. In *Gideon v Wainwright*, the court held that the assistance of counsel was a fundamental right essential to a fair trial. It is guaranteed by the U.S. Constitution to all defendants charged with a serious crime.

From a Florida Poolroom to the Supreme Court

Clarence Earl Gideon had a hard life. Born in 1910, he ran away from home at 14. He spent time in a reformatory, got married, and had a child. When he was 18, he got into trouble again and was sentenced to prison for three years. He spent the next 33 years working at odd jobs, gambling, and going in and out of jail for occasional thefts. In 1961, he was arrested for breaking into the Bay Harbor Poolroom in Panama City, Florida. Charged with a felony, Gideon appeared in court without funds and without a

 Landmarks: Historic U.S. Supreme Court Decisions

lawyer. He asked the judge to appoint a lawyer
for him, but the judge denied his request. The
judge stated that under Florida state law, the
court could only appoint counsel for a person
charged with a capital offense.

Gideon responded: "The United States Supreme
Court says I am entitled to be represented by counsel." At trial Gideon conducted his own defense.
He cross-examined the state's witnesses and made a
short argument emphasizing his innocence. But
the jury returned a guilty verdict, and he was sentenced to serve five years in state prison.

It was from prison that Gideon prepared two
documents, written in pencil on lined sheets of
paper, which he put into a large envelope and
sent to the U.S. Supreme Court. The first was a
motion to proceed *in forma pauperis*. (The phrase
is Latin for "in the form of a pauper.") If granted, this allows a person to proceed in federal
court without paying the filing fee or filing multiple copies of printed forms. The second was a
five-page document titled "Petition for Writ of
Certiorari." A writ of certiorari is a legal motion
to bring a case to the Supreme Court from a
lower court. In his handwritten petition, Gideon
claimed that the trial court's refusal to grant his
request for counsel had deprived him of due
process of law.

The Supreme Court receives far more petitions
for certiorari each year than it can hear. In 1961,
only about 150 petitions were granted out of
more than 2,500 that were filed. And only 3 percent of *in forma pauperis* motions were granted.
But the legal issue that Gideon raised was one
that had gained increasing importance to judges
and prosecutors around the country. To rule in
his favor would mean overruling a prior decision
of the court—the 1942 case of *Betts v. Brady*. But
in the 20 years since the *Betts* decision, there had
been increasing criticism of that ruling in the
legal community. Thus on June 4, 1962, the
Supreme Court granted Gideon's request for a hearing and issued an order stating that counsel should
discuss in their briefs: "Should this Court's holding
in *Betts v Brady* . . . be reconsidered?"

Is the Assistance of Counsel Necessary to a Fair Trial?

The Sixth Amendment guarantees a number of
rights to a criminal defendant:

> In all criminal prosecutions, the accused
> shall enjoy the right to a speedy and public
> trial, by an impartial jury . . . and to be
> informed of the nature and cause of the
> accusation; to be confronted with the witness-
> es against him; to have compulsory process
> for obtaining witnesses in his favor, and to
> have the Assistance of Counsel for his
> defence.

But in 1833, the Supreme Court in *Barron v
Baltimore* held that the Bill of Rights only
applied to the federal government, not to the
states. Thus the Sixth Amendment right to counsel only applied to defendants in federal courts.

By 1932, every state had passed laws requiring a
trial judge to appoint a lawyer for criminal defendants in capital cases—and in some states, also
for defendants charged with other serious crimes.
But often trial judges failed to follow those laws.
That was what happened in *Powell v. Alabama*.
That case came to the U.S. Supreme Court after
seven defendants had been found guilty and sentenced to death. They had appealed to the
Alabama Supreme Court, but their appeal was
denied. The defendants then appealed to the U.S.
Supreme Court, claiming that the trial court's
failure to provide them with legal assistance was a
violation not of the Sixth Amendment, but of
the due process clause of the 14th Amendment.

The *Powell* case involved a horrifying set of circumstances. The seven defendants were young
African Americans who had been traveling on a
freight train in Alabama. Also on the train were
seven young white men and two white women.
After a fight, the white men (and the two
women), claimed that the women had been
raped. As soon as the train reached the station,
the defendants were arrested by a sheriff's posse
and taken to jail. Within a few days, they were
tried and sentenced to death.

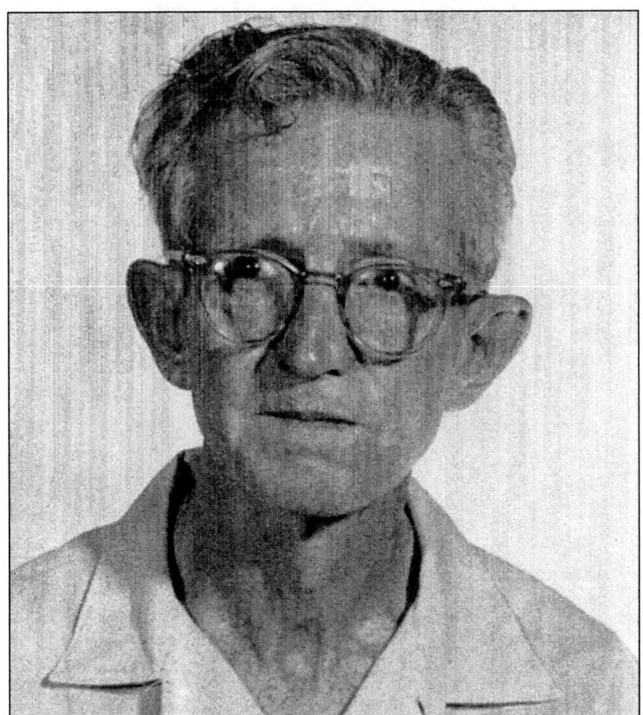

Clarence Earl Gideon (1910-1972) did not have enough money to pay for a lawyer and none was provided to him. Convicted of a felony, he submitted a handwritten petition for certiorari to the U.S. Supreme Court.

In its ruling, the Supreme Court held that the right to a hearing and a fair trial were among the "fundamental rights and principles" that "lie at the base of all our civil and political institutions." A denial of those rights would violate the 14th Amendment's guarantee of "due process of law." In light of the facts of the case, "the ignorance and illiteracy of the defendants, their youth, the circumstances of public hostility . . . and above all that they stood in deadly peril of their lives," the court ruled that the trial court's failure to give the defendants effective assistance of counsel made a fair trial impossible and "was a clear denial of due process."

The court clearly believed that *no* person can have a fair trial without the assistance of a lawyer. "Even the intelligent and educated layman," the court wrote, has "no skill in the science of law." Such a person does not know how to prepare his defense, and "though he be not guilty he faces the danger of conviction because he does not know how to establish his innocence." But the court limited its decision. It only applied to

death sentence cases, where the defendant "is incapable of adequately making his own defense because of ignorance, feeble-mindedness, illiteracy or the like." Whether the failure to appoint counsel would be a denial of due process "in other criminal prosecutions or under other circumstances, we need not determine."

Betts v Brady—No 'Hard and Fast Rule'

In 1942, 10 years after the *Powell* decision, the Supreme Court again considered the issue of a defendant's right to counsel. The defendant in *Betts v. Brady* was charged in Maryland state court with robbery. Because he had no money, he could not hire a lawyer. He asked the court to appoint one for him. The court refused, and Betts pleaded not guilty and conducted his own defense. He was found guilty and sentenced to eight years in prison. Betts, like Gideon, filed a petition to the U.S. Supreme Court. He argued that under the holding of the *Powell* case, the state court's refusal to grant his request for a lawyer denied him due process, in violation of the 14th Amendment.

The Supreme Court disagreed. It stated that the concept of due process was not easily defined. Not having legal counsel could in one case result in a "denial of fundamental fairness, shocking to the universal sense of justice," but in other cases, it would not be a denial of due process. The court also reviewed the rules adopted in each state. It determined that in many states the appointment of counsel was not considered to be a fundamental right essential to a fair trial. Each state, the court noted, has the power to appoint counsel where it believes it necessary in the interest of fairness. The court was unwilling to create a set of "hard and fast rules" obligating the states to furnish counsel in every case.

As for the facts in the *Betts* case, the court relied on the trial judge. He had found that Betts was 43 years old, of ordinary intelligence, and able to take care of his own interests at trial. Based on those facts, the Supreme Court upheld Betts'

Landmarks: Historic U.S. Supreme Court Decisions

conviction. The due process clause of the 14th Amendment, the court ruled, does not mean that a defendant cannot receive a fair trial without a lawyer. "As we have said, the Fourteenth Amendment prohibits the conviction and incarceration of one whose trial is offensive to the common and fundamental ideas of fairness and right," and while "want of counsel may result in a conviction lacking in such fundamental fairness" that is not always the case.

Not all the justices agreed with the court's opinion. Justice Hugo Black issued a strong dissent, joined by two other justices. It quoted the *Powell* decision about the need for a lawyer and how even an "intelligent and educated layman" lacks to ability to prepare his own defense. Innocent people, the dissenters wrote, should not be subjected to an increased danger of conviction just because of poverty. Most states, Justice Black wrote, do provide that poor defendants be given the assistance of counsel *in all criminal cases.* "Any other practice seems to me to defeat the promise of our democratic society to provide equal justice under law."

Gideon v Wainwright—One Rule For All Felony Cases

The decision in the *Betts* case created a "special circumstances" test to determine if refusing a defendant's request for a lawyer would deny due process. The formula that *state* courts had to use was whether a trial without a lawyer would offend the "fundamental ideas of fairness and right." But applying that formula proved to be almost impossible for trial courts. Many cases of defendants tried without lawyers were brought to the Supreme Court in the 20 years after the *Betts* decision. In almost every case, the court found that "special circumstances" did exist and that due process had been denied. Those cases were remanded to the state for retrial.

The attorney who represented Gideon before the Supreme Court was Abe Fortas, one of the most prominent lawyers in the country. (He later became a Supreme Court justice in 1965.) Because

Known as possessing one of the best legal minds in the nation, Abe Fortas (1910–1982) was appointed to represent Gideon before the Supreme Court. Fortas later served as a justice of the Supreme Court from 1965 to 1969.

the *Betts* decision had evoked so much criticism from trial lawyers and judges, Fortas felt confident that he could persuade a majority of the justices to rule that the 14th Amendment required states to provide a lawyer to all defendants in felony cases. But Fortas wanted more than just a majority; he wanted a unanimous decision.

One argument he used was that a "hard and fast rule" requiring all states to provide counsel would give states more independence. It would require little oversight and interference from the federal government. Since 1950, the Supreme Court had heard an increasing number of appeals from state prisoners who did not have legal assistance at their trials. In most of those cases, the court had ruled in favor of the prisoner and against the state. Fortas argued that the doctrine of federalism required the court to overturn its decision in *Betts* and put in place a simple rule that would stop the federal government from intruding on the states. Fortas was joined in this argument by the attorneys general of 22 states, who filed a brief arguing that the *Betts* case should be overturned.

Perhaps the biggest challenge that Fortas faced was the doctrine of stare decisis. "Stare decisis" is Latin meaning to stand by things decided. Under the rule of stare decisis, the Supreme Court tries not to overturn its own decisions unless it has a strong reason to do so. In this instance, however, many reasons seemed to exist. Increasing numbers of states already required that counsel be provided in felony trials. Many experienced defense lawyers agreed that murder cases were not always the most difficult to defend. If due process required that counsel be provided in murder cases, it should therefore require that lawyers represent defendants in felony cases where the defendant faced prison for 20 or 30 years. And the *Betts* decision was increasingly being criticized as unfair to the poor. Just a year before the *Gideon* case, Justice William O. Douglas wrote that refusing the right to counsel in every case seemed to him to be a denial of equal protection. "Certainly he who has a long purse will always have a lawyer, while the indigent will be without one. I know of no more invidious discrimination based on poverty."

For all those reasons, the nine justices of the court unanimously agreed that *Betts v. Brady* had been wrongly decided. The court returned to the conclusion that it had reached in the *Powell* case: A fair trial requires legal assistance. "Reason and reflection," it stated, "require us to recognize that in our adversary system of criminal justice, any person hauled into court, who is too poor to hire a lawyer, cannot be assured a fair trial unless it is provided for him." The *Betts* case, it said, "was an anachronism when handed down" and should now be overruled.

Gideon's case was remanded to the State of Florida. Five months later Gideon was retried in Panama City state court and represented by an attorney. Trial commenced at 10 a.m. The jury went out at 4:20 p.m., and one hour later returned with a verdict of not guilty. After two years in the state penitentiary, Clarence Earl Gideon was free.

Later Developments

The *Gideon* case involved a felony, a serious crime punishable by a year or more in state prison. Nine years later, in *Argersinger v. Hamlin*, the Supreme Court expanded the scope of the ruling. It held that no person could be imprisoned "for any offense, whether classified as petty, misdemeanor or felony, unless he was represented by counsel at trial." Thus, when defendants are charged with a crime and their liberty is in jeopardy, they have a constitutional right to legal counsel.

These decisions revolutionized the criminal defense bar. Historically, most defense attorneys were private attorneys who required payments from their clients. With the decisions in *Gideon* and subsequent cases, the government had to provide lawyers to defendants who could not afford attorneys. The federal government, states, and counties set up systems to do this. In many places today, courts appoint private council, paid by the government, to represent those who cannot afford lawyers. In large cities, public defenders, employed by the government, provide legal counsel to criminal defendants.

For Discussion

1. What is the adversary system? Why do you think attorneys are important to this system?

2. What was the *Powell* case about? How did the Supreme Court rule in this case? How did it limit its ruling?

3. What was the *Betts* case about? How did the Supreme Court rule?

4. How were the *Betts* and *Gideon* cases similar? What is stare decisis? Do you think it is an important principle? Explain.

5. Why do you think Gideon's attorney wanted a unanimous decision? What arguments did he use to get unanimity? Do you agree with them? Explain.

6. What was the court's decision in *Gideon*? Do you agree with it? Explain. How did the court later expand this decision?

Landmarks: Historic U.S. Supreme Court Decisions

A Civil *Gideon*?

The Sixth Amendment is the only place in the Constitution that expressly mentions the right to an attorney. This amendment concerns criminal trials. Thus the Constitution is silent on the right to counsel in non-criminal, or civil, cases.

The Fifth and 14th amendments, however, guarantee due process of law. Due process mandates fundamental fairness in trials—both civil and criminal. Due process clearly allows parties to a lawsuit to have attorneys. The question is whether in civil cases it guarantees legal counsel to defendants who cannot afford lawyers.

In 1981 in *Lassiter v. Department of Social Services*, the U.S. Supreme Court decided such a case. The Department of Social Services had gained custody of the defendant's neglected child. A year later, the defendant was convicted of second-degree murder and sentenced to prison. While she was in prison, the department petitioned state court to terminate the defendant's parental rights. The court granted the department's petition after a hearing. The defendant took part in the hearing, but she did not have a lawyer (she said she could not afford one). The defendant appealed, claiming the due process clause of the 14th amendment required that the state provide her a lawyer in this case. In a 5–4 decision, the court ruled against her. The court recognized that due process may require a lawyer be appointed in some civil cases. It said, however, that the basic rule is that "there is a right to appointed counsel only where the indigent, if he is unsuccessful, may lose his personal freedom." But a court must evaluate three additional factors:

1. The "private interests at stake." In this case, the defendant had a strong interest in keeping her rights as a parent.

2. The "government's interest." The government had a strong interest in protecting the child.

3. The "risk that the procedures used will lead to erroneous decisions." This factor assesses the complexity of the case and the need for a lawyer. In this case, the court decided that the case was straightforward and presented no difficult issues of law.

These factors must strongly weigh against following the basic rule. In this case, the court concluded the factors did not mandate any change in the basic rule.

Since this decision, the Supreme Court has not ruled on another case asking for attorneys to be provided in civil cases. But many states have enacted laws requiring indigent defendants to be provided lawyers in certain civil cases.

Imagine that your group is a subcommittee to your state's Senate Judiciary Committee. You are to recommend in each type of civil case below whether the state should provide attorneys to indigent defendants.

As a group, read and discuss each type of case listed below. For each, do the following:

1. Decide whether to recommend that the state provide attorneys to indigent defendants in such cases. To help you decide, discuss the three factors the Supreme Court mentioned in the *Lassiter* case.

2. Be prepared to make your recommendation to the class and back it with reasons.

Types of Cases

Child custody. A defendant in this type of case is likely to lose custody of the child to the other parent. In some custody cases, the state attempts to remove the child from the defendant and place the child in foster care.

Eviction. Defendants in this type of case face being thrown out of their homes.

Civil asset forfeiture. This is a type of legal procedure allowed in certain types of criminal cases, typically drug cases. It is a civil (not a criminal) action against property involved in a crime. Technically, the property is the defendant, not the owner. (Thus strange case names result. For example: *State v. One 1990 Ford Thunderbird*, *State v. Ten Acres of Land*, or *State v. U.S. Currency in the Amount of $3,743*.) If the owners of the property can prove that they did not know about the illegal activity, they will not lose the property.

Miranda v. Arizona (1966)

'You Have the Right to Remain Silent . . . .'

In everyday encounters with people, police do not have to issue *Miranda* warnings. But if they take a suspect into custody, they must read the suspect *Miranda* warnings and obtain a waiver before questioning the suspect.

In the 1960s, two currently well-known government warnings first came into use. One appears on every pack of cigarettes and warns against smoking. The other is issued to criminal suspects before questioning by police:

> You have the right to remain silent. Anything you say can and will be used against you in a court of law. You have the right to an attorney. If you cannot afford an attorney, one will be provided for you.

This latter warning grew out of the highly controversial 1966 Supreme Court decision of *Miranda v. Arizona*. The court ruled that the Fifth Amendment to the U.S. Constitution required police to issue this warning before questioning suspects in custody.

The Fifth Amendment, in part, says that "(no) person . . . shall be compelled in any criminal case to be a witness against himself. . . ." The Supreme Court did not rule that the Fifth Amendment applied to the states until 1964. But even before this, it struck down cases where confessions were not made voluntarily. The court determined that these cases violated the due process clause of the 14th Amendment. This clause declares that no "State shall deprive any person of life, liberty, or property, without due process of law. . . ." Due process of law guarantees fair procedures and basic liberties.

A witness identified Ernesto Miranda, number 1, from this lineup after his arrest in 1963.

Over the years the Supreme Court struck down many state court cases as violating due process. The court ruled that confessions were coerced in the following situations:

- Deputies whipped the defendant and threatened not to stop until he confessed (*Brown v. Mississippi*, 1936).

- Police hid the defendant from his friends and attorney and questioned him continuously for three days (*Ward v. Texas*, 1942).

- Police questioned the suspect for 36 hours with only one five-minute break (*Ashcraft v. Tennessee*, 1944).

- Police took the defendant to a hotel room instead of jail, stripped him, and questioned him for three hours while he was naked (*Malinski v. New York*, 1945).

- Police questioned the defendant for days allowing him little sleep, brought in a doctor trained in hypnosis, wired the room so they could listen in, and had the doctor repeatedly suggest that the defendant confess (*Leyra v. Denno*, 1954).

- Police ignored the defendant's request for his lawyer and questioned him for eight straight hours, finally sending in a childhood friend, a policeman with four children, who falsely told the defendant he would be fired unless the defendant confessed (*Spano v. New York*, 1959).

- Police told the defendant that if she confessed, nothing would happen to her, but if she did not, her children would be taken away from her (*Lynum v. Illinois*, 1963).

Finally in 1964 in *Malloy v. Hogan*, the Supreme Court ruled that the Fifth Amendment protection against self-incrimination applied to the states. But courts still faced the difficult task of determining on a case-by-case basis whether confessions were coerced or voluntary. So in 1966 in the landmark case of *Miranda v. Arizona*, the Supreme Court laid down clearer guidelines for police and courts to follow.

Miranda v. Arizona (1966)

In this case, Ernesto Miranda was suspected of kidnapping and rape. Police arrested him at his home and took him to the police station. A witness identified him, and two detectives took him into a special room. After two hours of interrogation, the officers got Miranda to sign a written confession.

At his trial, Miranda was convicted of kidnaping and rape and was sentenced to 20 to 30 years in prison. But police had never told him of his Fifth Amendment right not to talk to them.

Writing for the five-member majority, Chief Justice Earl Warren stressed that the Fifth Amendment does not just apply to criminal trials. Its command that no person "shall be compelled in any criminal case to be a witness against himself" also applies to suspects in police custody. Any confession made to police must be voluntarily made. The court quoted from a unanimous 1924 Supreme Court decision that itself was citing an 1897 decision:

> . . . voluntariness is not satisfied by establishing merely that the confession was not induced by a promise or a threat. A confession is voluntary in law if, and only if, it was, in fact, voluntarily made. A confession may have been given voluntarily, although it was made to police officers, while in custody, and in answer to an examination conducted by them. But a confession obtained by compulsion must be excluded . . . .

Warren's opinion examined what made a confession coerced. One method of coercing a confession is through physical brutality. But, quoting another Supreme Court decision, the court stressed that:

> ". . . coercion can be mental as well as physical, and . . . the blood of the accused is not the only hallmark of an unconstitutional inquisition." . . . Interrogation still takes place in privacy. Privacy results in secrecy and this in turn results in a gap in our knowledge as to what in fact goes on in the interrogation rooms.

The court looked at interrogation techniques taught in police manuals. The techniques the court cited ranged from having false witnesses identify the defendant to police officers playing "good-cop, bad-cop." The court summed up the techniques as getting the suspect alone, depriving "him of any outside support. The aura of confidence in his guilt undermines his will to resist. . . . Patience and persistence, at times relentless questioning, are employed."

The court concluded "that without proper safeguards," police questioning of suspects in custody "contains inherently compelling pressures which work to undermine the individual's will to resist and to compel him to speak where he would not otherwise do so freely." The court decided that any interrogation of a suspect in custody is unconstitutional unless the police have clearly issued these warnings to the suspect:

- You have the right to remain silent.

- Anything you say may be used against you in court.

- You have a right to a lawyer.

- If you want a lawyer but can't afford one, the court will appoint one before any questioning.

Also, after giving a suspect these warnings, the police may not go on interrogating unless suspects "knowingly and intelligently" waive their rights. That is, suspects must completely understand their rights before they can give them up. This meant that if police did not give suspects in custody these warnings before questioning them, nothing that they said could be introduced as evidence against them at their trials.

The court left open the possibility that Congress or state legislatures could modify the procedures set forth in the opinion. But the new procedures must be "at least as effective in apprising accused persons of the right of silence and in assuring a continuous opportunity to exercise it. . . ."

Landmarks: Historic U.S. Supreme Court Decisions

The Dissenters

Four members of the court dissented and wrote three separate dissents. They saw no reason for adopting new rules on confessions. They believed the court should continue to review confessions individually to determine whether they were coerced.

> The new rules are not designed to guard against police brutality or other unmistakably banned forms of coercion. Those who use third-degree tactics and deny them in court are equally able and destined to lie as skillfully about warnings and waivers.

Historically, they argued, the Fifth Amendment did not apply to confessions. It was meant to protect against a defendant being forced to testify in court.

Finally, the dissenters believed the court was unwise in discouraging confessions.

> The obvious underpinning of the Court's decision is a deep-seated distrust of all confessions. . . . I see nothing wrong or immoral, and certainly nothing unconstitutional, in the police's asking a suspect whom they have reasonable cause to arrest whether or not he killed his wife or in confronting him with the evidence on which the arrest was based, at least where he has been plainly advised that he may remain completely silent . . . . Particularly when corroborated . . . such confessions have the highest reliability and significantly contribute to the certitude with which we may believe the accused is guilty. Moreover, it is by no means certain that the process of confessing is injurious to the accused. To the contrary it may provide psychological relief and enhance the prospects for rehabilitation.

Miranda's Aftermath

Ernesto Miranda's conviction was reversed. He was retried, without his confession being admitted into evidence, and convicted again.

The majority opinion indicated that defense attorneys would be more involved in custodial interrogations. The dissenters predicted that confessions would "markedly decrease." Neither prediction came to pass. Many suspects waive their rights and talk to police without attorneys. The number of confessions has not declined.

For Discussion

1. The Fifth Amendment's protection against self-incrimination did not always apply to the states. The article gives examples of seven cases (on page 62) where the Supreme Court ruled that the confessions obtained violated due process of law (guaranteed by the 14th Amendment). Do you agree that each of these cases violated due process? Explain.

2. What did the court decide in *Miranda*? What were the reasons for the decision? What reasons did the dissenters give against the decision? Do you agree with the majority opinion? Explain.

3. When do police have to give *Miranda* warnings? Do you think people should be considered in custody when police pull them over for a traffic stop? When they are briefly stopped and frisked for weapons? Explain.

4. When *Miranda* was decided, its critics claimed that suspects would stop making confessions. This claim has proved false. Do you think *Miranda* sufficiently protects suspects' Fifth Amendment rights? Do you think it goes too far? Explain.

A C T I V I T Y

Interpreting *Miranda*

The Supreme Court has made many decisions interpreting the *Miranda* decision. For example, *Miranda* requires the police to read suspects **in custody** their rights before any interrogation. Police do not need to get people to waive their rights if they are not in custody. The court has clarified what "in custody" means. To be in custody, a person's freedom must be significantly restrained. The court has held that most people stopped briefly by police are not in custody, because they will soon be on their way. Thus routine traffic stops and even "stop and frisks" (when officers briefly stop people and pat them down for weapons) do not normally require *Miranda* warnings.

In this activity, you will role play attorneys and members of the U.S. Supreme Court, arguing and deciding three important decisions actually heard by the Supreme Court. Your teacher will assign your group one of the cases on the next pages and also will assign each group member one of the following roles: Supreme Court justice, defense attorney, or prosecutor.

Instructions for Supreme Court Justices

Preparing for the Argument

1. Read your assigned case.

2. Think about the issue before the court. Review the *Miranda* decision and with other justices discuss how *Miranda* and the Fifth Amendment might apply to this case.

3. Think up questions to ask the prosecution and defense attorneys.

Conducting the Oral Argument

You will be in charge of hearing arguments from both sides of the case. Each side should get an equal amount of time. You can interrupt at any time to ask questions. This happens all the time in actual oral argument before the court. Ask both sides to answer your questions.

Ask each side to introduce themselves and tell who they represent.

The petitioner should be the first to argue. (The petitioner is the side that lost in appellate court and is named first in the case name.)

The respondent should argue second. (The respondent is the side that won in appellate court and is named last in the case name.)

Give both sides an opportunity to respond to each other's arguments.

Deciding the Case

After hearing the arguments, think about them and also about how *Miranda* and the Fifth Amendment apply to your case. Decide the issue presented in the case. Be prepared to give reasons for your decision.

Instructions for Attorneys

You are responsible for presenting the court with sound arguments for your side.

Preparing for the Argument

1. Read your assigned case.

2. Think about the issue before the court. Be sure of which side you are arguing.

3. Review the *Miranda* decision and with other attorneys on the same side and discuss how *Miranda* and the Fifth Amendment apply to this case.

4. Think up arguments that support your side. Be prepared to answer questions from justices and to counter arguments that the other side may present.

At Oral Argument

State your name and who you represent. When asked to present an argument, do so clearly and strongly, but courteously. Do not interrupt the other side.

Landmarks: Historic U.S. Supreme Court Decisions

Cases

#1: *Rhode Island v. Innis* (1980). *Miranda* requires the police to read suspects **in custody** their rights before any **interrogation**. This case brought forth the question of what interrogation means. Innis was arrested on suspicion of using a shotgun to rob a taxi driver a few hours earlier. Although he was arrested while still on the street, no weapon was found in his possession. He was given his *Miranda* warnings, and he requested to speak with a lawyer before any questioning. Three police officers were in the car transporting Innis to the police station. They began a conversation among themselves about how it would be too bad if children attending a nearby school for the handicapped found the abandoned shotgun that Innis had supposedly used in the robbery. Innis spoke up and directed the officers to the gun. Innis was indicted for kidnapping and armed robbery and for the murder of another taxi driver. Innis moved to suppress the prosecution's introduction into evidence of the shotgun and his statements made to police officers. The trial court, however, allowed them in, and he was convicted of all charges. On appeal, the Rhode Island Supreme Court reversed his conviction, saying the trial court erred in allowing the evidence because Innis had asked for a lawyer before being questioned and the police had ignored this and engaged in interrogation on the way to the station. The prosecution requested certiorari from the U.S. Supreme Court. The issue before the Supreme Court: Did the officers' conversation amount to interrogation?

#2: *New York v. Quarles* (1984). Police chased Quarles, a rape suspect, through a supermarket. Finally catching and handcuffing him, they found he had an empty shoulder holster. An officer asked him where the gun was. Nodding toward some empty boxes, Quarles said, "The gun is over there." The police retrieved a loaded .38 caliber handgun from a box. Quarles was charged with illegal possession of a gun. At trial, the judge excluded Quarles's statement and the gun from evidence because Quarles was not given *Miranda* warnings before being questioned. The prosecution appealed, claiming the *Miranda* rule should not apply in an emergency situation given the gun's danger to the public. The New York Appellate Division and Court of Appeals both rejected the prosecution's argument and affirmed the trial court's decision. The U.S. Supreme Court granted certiorari. The issue before the court: Should there be a public safety exception to the *Miranda* rule?

#3: *Dickerson v. U.S.* **(2000).** Under questioning by federal agents, Dickerson admitted driving the getaway car in a series of bank robberies. Dickerson later claimed he had not been given his *Miranda* warnings, and the trial court therefore ruled his confession could not be used in evidence. The prosecution appealed. The appellate court ruled that since Dickerson's confession was voluntary, it could be admitted under Section 3501 of the U.S. Code, a federal law that was more than 30 years old. Enacted by Congress, Section 3501 responded to the *Miranda* case by permitting a confession in federal cases to be admitted in evidence "if it is voluntarily given." Thus the law returned to the voluntariness test that existed before *Miranda*. For 30 years, prosecutors and police had ignored this law. The U.S. Supreme Court granted certiorari. The issue before the U.S. Supreme Court: Is this law constitutional?

The relevant parts of the Section 3501 read as follows:

(a) In any criminal prosecution brought by the United States . . . a confession . . . shall be admissible in evidence if it is voluntarily given. . . .

(b) The trial judge in determining the issue of voluntariness shall take into consideration all the circumstances surrounding the giving of the confession, including (1) the time elapsing between arrest and arraignment of the defendant making the confession, if it was made after arrest and before arraignment, (2) whether such defendant knew the nature of the offense with which he was charged or of which he was suspected at the time of making the confession, (3) whether or not such defendant was advised or knew that he was not required to make any statement and that any such statement could be used against him, (4) whether or not such defendant had been advised prior to questioning of his right to the assistance of counsel; and (5) whether or not such defendant was without the assistance of counsel when questioned and when giving such confession.

The presence or absence of any of the above-mentioned factors to be taken into consideration by the judge need not be conclusive on the issue of voluntariness of the confession.

On August 9, 1974, President Nixon prepared to board a helicopter and depart from the White House after resigning. He extended his hand to Gerald Ford, his successor as president.

On July 24, 1974, the Supreme Court issued a unanimous decision in *U.S. v. Nixon*. The court upheld an order requiring President Richard Nixon to produce tapes of 64 conversations with four of his top aides. One of those tapes—the "smoking gun"—resulted in a firestorm of indignation in Congress and throughout the nation. Two days later, the House Judiciary Committee voted to impeach the president. On August 9, the president resigned—the first president in U.S. history to do so.

The Special Prosecutor's Quest for Tapes

The decision in *U.S. v. Nixon* followed a year of political and legal controversy over the powers of a "special prosecutor" appointed to investigate an unusual burglary. Early in 1972 (an election year) five men had been caught breaking into the Democratic Party headquarters in the Watergate building in Washington, D.C. The FBI discovered that the burglars were tapping telephones and that they were being paid with money from the Republican Committee to Re-Elect the President. President Richard Nixon and his top aides denied any knowledge of the break-in. Nixon ordered the attorney general to appoint a special prosecutor to uncover the facts surrounding the Watergate burglary.

Archibald Cox, the special prosecutor, began his investigation in May 1973. By then, the burglars had already been indicted and had pleaded guilty. Evidence had also been uncovered that the White House was involved with the break-in and had authorized the payment of "hush money" (and perhaps a promise of clemency) to make sure that the burglars wouldn't talk.

A Senate committee was also investigating Watergate and the cover-up. Some of Nixon's top aides who testified before the Senate denied knowing of the break-in or of a cover-up. But others, and particularly the president's counsel, John Dean, told of a cover-up. If what John Dean told the Senate was true, the president and his aides were guilty of obstructing justice and other crimes.

A bombshell fell on July 13, 1973. A witness told the Senate investigating committee that the president had installed a tape recorder in his office in early 1971. All his conversations had been recorded. The tapes were likely the only way to resolve the ongoing disputes over the credibility of conflicting witnesses. Both the special prosecutor and the Senate committee asked the president to turn over the tapes. The president, however, refused. He claimed that "executive privilege" protected these conversations. He cited the need to encourage candor in discussions between him and his advisors. The privilege, he said, was constitutionally based and absolute.

Assigned to investigate the break-in and suspected cover-up, Special Prosecutor Cox believed obtaining the tapes was critical. Cox subpoenaed the tapes. (A subpoena is a court order for a person to appear in court or to produce evidence for the court.) The president asked Cox to drop the subpoena. Cox refused. On October 20, 1973, Nixon ordered Attorney General Elliot Richardson to fire Cox. Richardson refused and resigned. Nixon ordered the deputy attorney general to fire Cox. He also refused and resigned. The third in command at the Justice Department, Solicitor General Robert Bork, obeyed Nixon's order and fired Cox. This event became known as the "Saturday Night Massacre."

It caused a political uproar, and Nixon was forced to appoint a new special prosecutor a week later. The new special prosecutor, Leon Jaworski, continued the quest for the tapes.

Early in 1974, two months after Jaworski was appointed, a grand jury indicted seven former Nixon aides for conspiring to hinder the investigation of the Watergate burglary. (John Dean was one of those indicted.) The grand jury also named the president as an unindicted co-conspirator. Trial was set for September. In preparation, Jaworski obtained a court order demanding that the president produce 64 tapes believed to contain critical conversations between the president and the defendants. The president filed a motion to quash the order in District Court. The motion was denied. After the president filed an appeal in Circuit Court, the special prosecutor filed a petition asking the Supreme Court to take the case. The court granted the petition and heard arguments on July 8. Two weeks later, on July 24, 1974, Chief Justice Warren Burger delivered the court's unanimous decision. (Justice William Rehnquist did not participate in the decision. Before he was appointed to the court, he had worked with former Attorney General John Mitchell, one of the defendants.)

The President's Arguments

The president made two main arguments to the court. First, he argued that whether the tapes should be produced was simply an "intra-branch" matter—a dispute between two officers of the executive branch (himself and the special prosecutor). As head of the executive branch, the president should settle the dispute. Such a dispute, he contended, was not a matter for courts to decide. Writing for the unanimous court, Chief Justice Burger rejected this argument. Burger pointed out that a criminal trial was pending, and the dispute involved evidence that might be presented at trial. Therefore, Burger concluded, the dispute was clearly a matter for the courts.

The president's second argument relied on the doctrine of separation of powers. He argued that the tapes were subject to an "absolute"

    Landmarks: Historic U.S. Supreme Court Decisions

Rose Mary Woods, Nixon's secretary, demonstrated how she might have accidentally erased part of a tape important to the Watergate scandal.

privilege—one that is not limited—and should therefore not be turned over to the special prosecutor. The president's counsel argued that the president, as chief executive, had decided that tapes of confidential communications between himself and his advisors were privileged. The court, he said, should defer to the president's decision. The president's counsel argued that executive privilege was "part and parcel" of the separation of powers. He pointed out that the privilege "necessarily includes the right of the holder of the privilege to decide when it is to be exercised." The question, according to the president's counsel, was "who decides" when to exercise it. The answer, he argued, is "that it is for the Chief Executive, not for the judicial branch, to decide when the public interest permits disclosure of Presidential discussion."

The court disagreed. It held that interpreting the Constitution is part of the "Judicial Power of the United States." Article III of the Constitution vests this power in the judicial branch. Citing the 1962 Supreme Court case of *Baker v. Carr*, the court stated that deciding whether the Constitution commits a matter to Congress or to the executive "is a delicate exercise in Constitutional interpretation, and is a responsibility of this Court as ultimate interpreter of the Constitution." Or to put it more simply, citing *Marbury v. Madison*, it is "the province and duty of the judicial department to say what the law is."

Does the Constitution Provide an Executive Privilege?

"Executive privilege" was not mentioned in the Constitution. Nor was it discussed in the debates over the Constitution's adoption. In fact, the phrase was first coined in the 1950s. Even so, the Supreme Court found a constitutional basis for the claim of executive privilege. The privilege, according to the court, derives from the powers assigned to the executive branch. In carrying out the duties of the office, the president needs to protect the privacy of his communications with those who help him. It is clear, Chief Justice Burger wrote, that if the president's advisors think that their remarks could be made public, they might not be candid. This could hurt the decision-making process. The court stated: "Certain powers and privileges flow from the nature of enumerated powers; the protection of the confidentiality of Presidential communications has similar constitutional underpinnings."

While the court agreed with the president that a constitutionally based executive privilege exists, it did not agree that the privilege was absolute. In certain cases, involving military, diplomatic, or sensitive national-security secrets, the court implied that the president might have an unqualified privilege not to disclose information. (Even in such a case, a court would presumably examine the information to see whether it fit into one of these categories.) But in the case before the court, the privilege claimed for the tapes was based solely on a "broad, undifferentiated claim of the public interest in the confidentiality of conversations." The court held that where the basis for the claim of executive privilege was only the public interest in maintaining confidentiality, the privilege was not absolute but only "presumptive." In other words, the privilege could be overcome by an important countervailing interest.

Enforcing the Rule of Law

The countervailing interest here was the special prosecutor's need for the information. The court considered the weight of this claim. The subpoena for the tapes had been sought in the cases of seven former presidential aides, who would shortly stand trial. They would be tried under an adversarial criminal justice system in which the parties contest all issues before a court of law. The integrity of this system depends on full disclosure of facts. Compulsory process for the production of evidence is frequently necessary for courts to function. And just as the executive privilege is constitutionally based, so too are the rights of a criminal defendant. The Sixth

Amendment confers on every criminal defendant the right "to be confronted with the witnesses against him" and "to have compulsory process for obtaining witnesses in his favor." And the Fifth Amendment guarantees that no person shall be deprived of liberty "without due process of law."

The court weighed the two interests. On one side was the importance of the confidentiality of the president's communications. On the other side was the importance of preserving the integrity of the criminal justice system and the needs of the defendants who were awaiting trial. The court concluded that the demands of due process prevailed:

> We conclude that when the ground for asserting privilege as to subpoenaed materials sought for use in a criminal trial is based only on the generalized interest in confidentiality, it cannot prevail over the fundamental demands of due process in the fair administration of justice. The generalized assertion of privilege must yield to the demonstrated, specific need for evidence in a pending criminal trial.

The court affirmed the District Court's ruling and ordered the president to transmit the subpoenaed materials to that court.

The Legacy of *U.S. v. Nixon*

In the months leading up to the Supreme Court's decision, many people worried that the president might defy the court's ruling and refuse to turn over the tapes. The president had made public statements hinting at that possibility. And in oral argument, counsel for the president would not say whether the president would comply with the subpoena. Archibald Cox, the first special prosecutor, expressed fears that by filing suit he might have set in motion a process leading to the president defying the Supreme Court—"and getting away with it." When the White House announced within eight hours after the court's decision that it would comply, many people expressed tremendous relief and

71

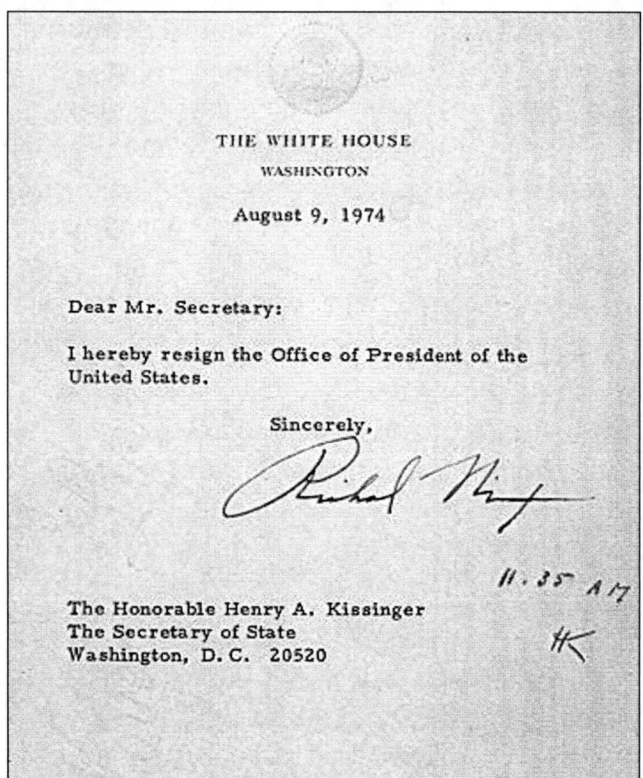

THE WHITE HOUSE
WASHINGTON

August 9, 1974

Dear Mr. Secretary:

I hereby resign the Office of President of the United States.

Sincerely,

Richard Nixon

11:35 AM

The Honorable Henry A. Kissinger
The Secretary of State
Washington, D.C. 20520

HK

President Nixon resigned from office by submitting this letter to Secretary of State Henry Kissinger.

satisfaction with the outcome. As one commentator noted, Nixon's decision to comply gave "crucial confirmation to the authority of the Court in our constitutional hierarchy."

The court's ruling reaffirmed the holding of *Marbury v. Madison*. When a constitutional question comes to court, the Supreme Court has the final word, and no one, including the president, is above the law.

It was a decision of tremendous political importance. The so-called "smoking gun tape" was made public on August 5, 1974. It showed that just days after the Watergate burglary, Nixon had met with his chief of staff and planned to use the CIA to block the FBI investigation. The tape's publication ended most of the president's political support. Facing impeachment, the president resigned on August 9.

From a legal point of view, however, the decision left several issues open. For example, the court did not indicate the weight it would give to executive confidentiality and to the public interest in civil lawsuits or in cases when Congress was seeking information. The court added in a footnote:

> We are not here concerned with the balance between the President's generalized interest in confidentiality and the need for relevant evidence in civil litigation, nor with that between the confidentiality interest and congressional demands for information, nor with the President's interest in preserving state secrets. (Footnote 19)

Thus, the decision did not say how the court might rule in a future dispute between Congress and the president over access to papers that the president does not want to disclose.

For Discussion

1. What do you think a special prosecutor is? Why do you think a special prosecutor was appointed in this case?

2. What was the struggle about between the president and special prosecutor? What was the Saturday Night Massacre? What was its result?

3. What trial set the stage for the Supreme Court confrontation between the president and special prosecutor? What did the special prosecutor want for the trial? Why?

4. What were the president's two main arguments to the court? How did the court answer them? Do you agree with the court's decisions? Why or why not?

5. What is executive privilege? How did the court and Nixon administration disagree on the privilege? Which do you think is right? Explain. The court balanced two interests in deciding whether to uphold the privilege. What were they? Do you think the court made the right decision in which interest prevailed? Why or why not?

6. What do you think is the greatest legacy of the case? Why?

Executive Privilege

The Supreme Court in *U.S. v. Nixon* for the first time ruled that executive privilege exists. But it ruled that it is a qualified privilege and not an absolute one. The court specifically did not rule on the balance between the president's need for confidentiality and (1) "the need for relevant evidence in civil litigation," (2) "congressional demands for information," or (3) the need to investigate secret information.

Imagine that you are legal advisors to the president. The president wants to invoke executive privilege in the three cases in the next column. Your task is to evaluate whether the Supreme Court would uphold a claim of executive privilege in each of these cases.

As a group, do the following:

1. Review the portions of the article on executive privilege. They can be found under the headings "Does the Constitution Provide an Executive Privilege?" and "Enforcing the Rule of Law."

2. Consider that the president has a "generalized interest in confidentiality" in each of the cases. Think about and write down what countervailing interests exist in each case.

3. Decide whether the countervailing interests in each case would be enough to overcome a claim of executive privilege.

4. Be prepared to report your decisions and reasons for them.

Cases

#1. Bondo Parcel Corporation is suing Zebra Parcel Corporation for stealing its secret customer list that it compiled over many years. Bondo has requested that the secretary of commerce testify as to conversations the secretary had with the CEO of Zebra. Citing executive privilege, the president has ordered the secretary not to testify at the civil lawsuit.

#2. The Senate Judiciary Committee is investigating whether the attorney general fired eight U.S. attorneys for political reasons. The committee has subpoenaed the former White House counsel and a former assistant to the attorney general. Citing executive privilege, the president has ordered them not to testify, and they have refused to testify.

#3. In the aftermath of a failed military action, the House Committee on Foreign Affairs is investigating what went wrong and why. It has subpoenaed outside advisors who met with the president before the military action. The House committee wants to ask them what they told the president. Citing executive privilege, the president orders them not to testify, and they comply with the president's order.

Regents of U.C. v. Bakke (1978)

Is Affirmative Action Constitutional?

President Lyndon Johnson signed the historic Civil Rights Act of 1964. Right behind him was Martin Luther King Jr.

No state shall . . . deny to any person within its jurisdiction the equal protection of its laws.
—Equal protection clause of the 14th Amendment

The 14th Amendment was adopted in 1868, following the Civil War. Its equal protection clause was intended primarily to prevent racial discrimination against blacks. It would take almost 100 years, however, before the equal protection clause was enforced to prevent racial discrimination.

After the Civil War, federal troops occupied the South. Following a 12-year occupation, Southern states were left to govern themselves. These states began enacting Jim Crow laws, which made racial segregation legal. Blacks and whites had to use separate schools, hospitals, libraries, restaurants, hotels, bathrooms, and even drinking fountains. In 1896 in *Plessy v. Ferguson*, the U.S. Supreme Court ruled that these laws did not violate the equal protection clause of the 14th Amendment as long as the separate facilities were equal.

With the backing of the court's "separate but equal" doctrine, Jim Crow laws spread throughout the South. They stayed in effect until the 1950s and 1960s, when the civil rights movement launched an all-out campaign against them. In a series of court cases, the U.S. Supreme Court, beginning with *Brown v. Board of Education*, declared that racial segregation laws were "inherently unequal" and violated the equal protection clause. The U.S. Congress bolstered the equal protection clause by passing the 1964 Civil Rights Act, ensuring equal rights for all citizens.

Affirmative-Action Programs

Following the successes of the civil rights movement, concern arose that simply making discrimination illegal would not achieve equality of opportunity in the United States. President Lyndon Johnson expressed this concern in a speech in 1965:

> You do not wipe away the scars of centuries by saying: "Now, you are free to go where you want, do as you desire, and choose the leaders you please." You do not take a man who for years has been hobbled by chains, liberate him, bring him to the starting line of a race, saying, "You are free to compete with all the others," and still justly believe you have been completely fair . . . This is the next and more profound stage of the battle for civil rights. We seek not just freedom but opportunity—not just legal equity but human ability—not just equality as a right and a theory, but equality as a fact and as a result.

President Johnson issued an executive order requiring government contractors to "take affirmative action" to hire minority employees. Soon the government, industry, and educational institutions developed affirmative-action programs. These programs were designed to offer extra opportunities to disadvantaged minorities who had suffered discrimination in the past. Their goal was to increase the percentage of minorities in higher education, in professional schools, and in upper-level business positions.

One result of affirmative-action programs is that sometimes a minority applicant for a job or school admission will be preferred over white applicants with similar or even better qualifications. It is argued that this preference of minority applicants is justified, since the idea behind affirmative action is to make up for past disadvantages suffered by these minority groups.

When a person is admitted or hired because he or she is a member of a minority group, a classification has been made based on race or ethnic background. In such a case, a person has been discriminated against because he or she is not a member of a minority group. This favoring of minority applicants over others is sometimes called reverse discrimination.

Reverse discrimination poses a constitutional question: Does the equal protection clause outlaw it? The *Bakke* case was the first reverse discrimination case decided by the U.S. Supreme Court. It was a landmark decision that affected the rights of both minority and non-minority groups all over the country.

Regents of the University of California v. Allan Bakke

Allan Bakke, a white engineer, applied to the University of California's medical school at Davis in 1973 and 1974. The school turned him down both times. Angered, Bakke sued the U.C. Regents in California Superior Court demanding admission to the Davis medical school. He claimed he had been turned down only because the school set aside 16 of the 100 spots in each first-year class for minority students. Had the 16 spots not been saved, he said, he would have gained admission both times, as he was in the top 16 of those whites who were turned down and ahead of those minority students in the special program. These "special admissions programs," Bakke argued, constitute reverse discrimination and are illegal.

The trial court found that the medical school's special admissions program violated both the 14th Amendment's equal protection clause and Title VI of the 1964 Civil Rights Act. Because of the importance of the issue, the California Supreme Court heard the appeal directly from the trial court. In September 1976, the California Supreme Court agreed with Bakke's claims. Basing its ruling on the 14th Amendment, the court held that the equal protection clause required that "no applicant may be rejected because of his race, in favor of another who is less qualified, as measured by standards applied without regard to race." The University of California appealed this decision to the U.S. Supreme Court.

The Divided Court

The Supreme Court was deeply divided on the case. Two opposing camps of four justices each issued opinions. The court's decision was written by Justice Lewis Powell, a member of neither camp. He got justices from both camps to concur with and even join in parts of his opinion. They dissented from other parts.

The Brennan Opinion

Writing for one camp was Justice William Brennan. Joining Justice Brennan were Justices Marshall, White, and Blackmun.

Justice Brennan argued that the Davis program did not violate the equal protection clause. The equal protection clause demanded that the court carefully examine any government program that makes decisions based on race. To be permissible under the equal protection clause, the program must serve an important government purpose. Brennan concluded that the Davis program's "purpose of remedying the effects of past societal discrimination is . . . sufficiently important to justify the use of race-conscious admissions programs" to overcome "substantial and chronic" minority underrepresentation in the medical profession.

The Stevens Opinion

The other camp of four justices included Chief Justice Burger and Justices Stewart, Stevens, and Rehnquist. Justice John Paul Stevens wrote the opinion for this group.

Justice Stevens pointed out that even though the *Bakke* case presented an important constitutional issue, "Our settled practice . . . is to avoid . . . a constitutional issue if a case can be fairly decided on a statutory ground." Stevens stated that the decision should be based on Title VI of the 1964 Civil Rights Act. This law provided:

> No person in the United States shall, on the ground of race, color, or national origin, be excluded from participation in . . . any program or activity receiving Federal financial assistance.

Stevens cited congressional sponsors of the legislation. They said that the law was meant to be "color-blind" and ban all discrimination based on race.

Stevens noted that the Davis medical school received federal financial assistance and the school "excluded Bakke from participation in its program of medical education because of his race." He therefore concluded that the school's special program violated this law.

The Opinion of the Court

Justice Lewis Powell wrote the opinion of the court. He disagreed with Brennan's opinion that the Davis program met the requirements of the equal protection clause. But he also disagreed with Stevens' conclusion that admissions programs could never consider a person's race.

He first addressed Stevens' claim that Title VI specifically banned giving preferential treatment to disadvantaged minorities. Powell argued (as did Brennan) that Title VI simply meant that those receiving federal funds could not violate the limits of the 14th Amendment. Powell cited statements from many members of Congress during the debate on the bill. One of the sponsors of the bill stated: "Basically, there is a constitutional restriction against discrimination in the use of Federal funds; and title VI simply spells out the procedure to be used in enforcing that restriction."

Justice Powell next turned to the Constitution's equal protection clause. This clause makes any program using racial distinction "inherently suspect." To be upheld, the program must be "precisely tailored to serve a compelling governmental interest."

The University of California cited four purposes for its program. Powell examined each to see if it was a "compelling government interest," and if so, whether it was "precisely tailored" to serve that interest.

The first goal was to increase the number of "traditionally disfavored minorities in medical schools and in the medical profession." Powell rejected this goal as unconstitutional: "Preferring members of any one group for no reason other

Lewis Powell Jr. (1907–1998) was a justice of the Supreme Court from 1972 to 1987. He wrote the opinion of the court in the *Bakke* case.

than race or ethnic origin is discrimination for its own sake. This the Constitution forbids."

The second goal was to counter the effects of "societal discrimination." Powell rejected that goal as too "amorphous a concept of injury." He stated that the court had "never approved a classification that aids persons perceived as members of relatively victimized groups at the expense of other innocent individuals" without "findings of constitutional or statutory violations."

The third goal of the program was to increase the number of doctors who will practice medicine in underserved communities. Powell agreed that this could be a compelling state interest. But he found "virtually no evidence in the record indicating that [the] special admissions program is either needed or geared to promote that goal."

The fourth and final goal of the program was to create "an ethnically diverse student body." Powell found diversity a compelling interest for public universities. He agreed that "the 'nation's future depends upon leaders trained through wide exposure' to the ideas and mores of students as diverse as this Nation of many peoples." But

he found the Davis program "flawed" in creating a diverse student body:

> The diversity that furthers a compelling state interest encompasses a far broader array of qualifications and characteristics of which racial or ethnic origin is but a single though important element. Petitioner's special admissions program, focused solely on ethnic diversity, would hinder rather than further attainment of genuine diversity.

Powell argued that it was improper to set aside a certain number of seats for members of minority groups. This type of program does not let all the applicants compete against one another. But Powell stated that a public university could consider race or ethnicity as a "plus" factor. He explained:

> This kind of program treats each applicant as an individual in the admissions process. The applicant who loses out on the last available seat to another candidate receiving a "plus" on the basis of ethnic background will not have been foreclosed from all consideration for that seat simply because he was not the right color or had the wrong surname. It would mean only that his combined qualifications, which may have included similar nonobjective factors, did not outweigh those of the other applicant. His qualifications would have been weighed fairly and competitively, and he would have no basis to complain of unequal treatment under the Fourteenth Amendment.

Thus Powell's opinion affirmed the California Supreme Court's judgment that the Davis program was invalid under the 14th Amendment. But it reversed the California court's ruling that the 14th Amendment's due process clause prevented the school from ever considering an applicant's race.

Aftermath

Allan Bakke was admitted to the Davis medical school. The legal results of the case, however, were unclear for many years. The court was so divided that many legal observers believed

Landmarks: Historic U.S. Supreme Court Decisions

Powell's opinion meant little. But in 2003, the Supreme Court decided two affirmative-action cases using Powell's reasoning. It struck down in *Gratz v. Bollinger* the University of Michigan's admissions program that automatically gave members of minority groups added points toward admission (assuring every qualified minority of admission). But in *Grutter v. Bollinger* it upheld the university's law school admissions program, which allowed race as one of many "plus" factors.

For Discussion

1. What is the equal protection clause? What was its original purpose? Why was it not used for this purpose for almost 100 years?

2. What are affirmative-action programs? What do you think of President Johnson's justification for such programs in his 1965 speech (see page 75)?

3. What was the affirmative-action program in the *Bakke* case? Why did Bakke believe it was unfair? What were the decisions of the California trial court and California Supreme Court?

4. The U.S. Supreme Court was deeply divided in the case. What was the dissenting opinion of Justice Brennan? The concurring opinion of Justice Stevens? How did Justice Powell get to write the opinion of the Supreme Court?

5. What were the four compelling interests that the University of California cited for its affirmative-action program? Which did Justice Powell believe were actually compelling interests? Do you agree with him? Explain.

6. How did Powell justify a program that uses race only as a "plus" factor? Do you agree that such a program is constitutional? Explain.

Affirmative-Action Policy

Imagine that you are members of the board of regents of your state's public university system. In addition to undergraduate and graduate education, this system operates professional schools that prepare students to become lawyers, doctors, and dentists. The regents are re-evaluating the university's current affirmative-action programs for professional schools. The regents are considering the following options:

Option 1: Retain the current affirmative-action program. The current program allows university officials to use race and ethnicity as one factor in admissions. Other factors include college grades, admission test scores (Law School Admission Test, Medical College Admission Test, Dental Admission Test), and outside activities. Supporters of this policy note that this policy has resulted in a dramatic increase in the number of African Americans and Latinos in the system's professional schools.

Option 2: Adopt a color-blind policy. This would eliminate race as a factor in admissions. The only factors university officials could consider would be college grades, admission test scores (Law School Admission Test, Medical College Admission Test, Dental Admission Test), and outside activities. Supporters of this policy acknowledge that at first fewer African Americans and Latinos will be admitted to the professional schools, but say that this policy is fairer and will raise standards at the schools.

In your group, do the following:

1. Discuss each option and its pros and cons.

2. Decide which option to choose.

3. Be prepared to report your choice and your reasons for it.

Texas v. Johnson (1989)

Is There a Constitutional Right to Burn the American Flag?

The flag is one of the most widely recognized symbols of the United States.

I disapprove of what you say, but I will defend to the death your right to say it.
—Voltaire (1664–1778), French philosopher and writer

If there is a bedrock principle underlying the First Amendment, it is that the government may not prohibit the expression of an idea simply because society finds the idea itself offensive or disagreeable.

—William J. Brennan Jr. (1906–1997), justice of the U.S. Supreme Court

In 1988, the U.S. Supreme Court agreed to hear *Texas v. Johnson*. This case raised the question of whether the First Amendment protected the right of a protester to burn the American flag. Some argue that the right to burn the American flag is fundamental to the First Amendment's guarantee of freedom of speech. Others maintain that burning the flag constitutes a fundamental rejection of the system that protects freedom of speech, and they conclude that such conduct does not merit First Amendment protection. In *Texas v. Johnson*, the Supreme Court settled the issue as a matter of constitutional law. As a political issue, however, the debate over flag burning remains controversial.

Regulation of Speech Under the First Amendment

Although the First Amendment guarantees freedom of speech, the guarantee is not absolute. Oliver Wendell Holmes Jr., a justice on the U.S. Supreme Court in the early 20th century, described one limitation on First Amendment freedoms in the case of *Schenck v. U.S.* He noted: "The most stringent protection of free speech would not protect a man in falsely shouting fire in a theatre and causing a panic." The *Schenck* case announced the "clear and present danger" test: Speech may be restricted if the words used "create a clear and present danger that they will bring about the substantive evils that Congress has a right to prevent."

Another aspect of freedom of speech is expressive conduct (such as flag burning). The Supreme Court has grappled with whether laws banning expressive conduct are permissible under the First Amendment. In *U.S. v. O'Brien*, the court upheld O'Brien's conviction for burning his draft card during the Vietnam War, even though this constituted expressive conduct. In so doing, the court crafted a three-part test for the constitutionality of restrictions on expressive conduct:

1. The restriction must further an important or substantial government interest. In this case, the court found that the government had a strong interest in issuing draft cards to help raise an army for national defense.

2. That interest must be unrelated to the suppression of free expression. The court found that a proper purpose for outlawing the destruction of draft cards was to ease the draft process and had nothing to do with suppressing free speech.

3. The incidental restriction on First Amendment freedoms must be no greater than is essential to the furtherance of the stated government interest. The court found that the government had an interest in draft-age men carrying draft cards, and the court saw no other way for the government to protect this interest than outlawing their destruction.

Since the law passed all three parts of the test, it was upheld as constitutional.

Facts of the Case

In 1984, the Republican Party held its convention in Dallas, Texas. As it re-nominated President Ronald Reagan as its candidate for president, protesters outside the convention hall denounced the policies of the Reagan administration. One of the protesters was Gregory Lee Johnson. Johnson and other protesters marched through the streets of Dallas, spray-painting buildings and causing other property damage. At several points, the protesters paused to stage "die-ins" in an effort to demonstrate the consequences of a potential nuclear war. At the end of the protest, Johnson doused an American flag in kerosene and set it on fire. As the flag burned, fellow protesters chanted anti-American slogans such as "red, white, and blue, we spit on you, you stand for plunder, you will go under."

Desecrating an American flag was a criminal offense in Texas, as it was under federal law and in 48 of the 50 U.S. states. Johnson was arrested and charged with violating the Texas flag desecration law. The trial court convicted Johnson, sentencing him to one year in prison and fining him $2,000. A Texas appeals court reversed Johnson's conviction, and the U.S. Supreme Court agreed to hear the case.

The Issues

The Supreme Court in *U.S. v. O'Brien* had set three tests for any restriction on expressive conduct. For such a restriction to be constitutional, it had to pass all three tests. The court in *Texas v. Johnson* thus had to determine whether Texas could demonstrate:

1. Texas had an important or substantial government interest in prohibiting the desecration of the flag.

2. This interest was unrelated to the suppression of free expression.

3. Prohibiting the desecration of the flag was narrowly tailored to furthering this interest.

William J. Brennan Jr. (1906–1997) served as a justice for 34 years (from 1956 to 1990). In his career, he wrote 1,360 opinions, the second greatest number in the history of the Supreme Court.

Justice Brennan's Majority Opinion

Justice Brennan, writing for a narrow majority of five justices, held that laws against desecrating the American flag violated the First Amendment. He reasoned that burning an American flag conveyed a political message, an act lying at the core of the freedom of speech guaranteed by the First Amendment.

As a preliminary matter, Justice Brennan found that burning the flag in a political demonstration constituted "conduct 'sufficiently imbued with elements of communication,' to implicate the First Amendment."

Texas argued that it had two compelling governmental interests in regulating such expression: (1) preventing breaches of the peace that flag desecration may cause and (2) preserving the flag as a symbol of nationhood and national unity. Justice Brennan rejected Texas' argument on preventing breaches of the peace, because no breach of the peace occurred in this instance, and

because Johnson's actions did not incite imminent lawless action. Justice Brennan next wrote that the government interest in preserving the flag as a symbol of nationhood and national unity was related to the suppression of expression. It thus, he stated, did not meet the *O'Brien* test regarding incidental restrictions on expression.

Justice Brennan then turned to the part of the flag-burning statute that he found particularly objectionable. The Texas statute only criminalized flag burning done "in a way that the [flag burner] knows will seriously offend" others. In analyzing this language, Brennan relied on Justice Robert H. Jackson's famous description of "one of our society's defining principles." In *West Virginia State Board of Education v. Barnette*, Justice Jackson wrote, "If there is any fixed star in our constitutional constellation, it is that no official, high or petty, can prescribe what shall be orthodox in politics, nationalism, religion, or other matters of opinion or force citizens to confess by word or act their faith therein." Justice Brennan explained:

> If we were to hold that a State may forbid flag burning wherever it is likely to endanger the flag's symbolic role, but allow it wherever burning a flag promotes that role—as where, for example, a person ceremoniously burns a dirty flag—we would be saying that when it comes to impairing the flag's physical integrity, the flag itself may be used as a symbol . . . only in one direction. We would be permitting a State to "prescribe what shall be orthodox" by saying that one may burn the flag to convey one's attitude toward it and its referents only if one does not endanger the flag's representation of nationhood and national unity.

Justice Brennan also noted that creating a special exception to the First Amendment to permit the criminalization of flag burning could lead to similar exceptions, such as for burning state flags, copies of the presidential seal, the Constitution, or other venerated objects. The line that would be drawn between those objects protected by such exceptions and those not so protected would necessarily be arbitrary.

Finally, Justice Brennan argued:

> The way to preserve the flag's special role is not to punish those who feel differently about [nationhood and national unity]. It is to persuade them that they are wrong.

Brennan quoted Justice Louis D. Brandeis' concurring opinion in the 1927 case *Whitney v. California*. Justice Brandeis wrote, "If there be time to expose through discussion the falsehood and fallacies, to avert the evil by the processes of education, the remedy to be applied is more speech, not enforced silence." Justice Brennan concluded: "We do not consecrate the flag by punishing its desecration, for in doing so we dilute the freedom that this cherished emblem represents."

Justices Marshall, Blackmun, Scalia, and Kennedy joined Brennan's majority opinion.

Justice Kennedy's Concurring Opinion

Justice Anthony Kennedy, the newest member of the court in 1989, wrote an unusual concurring opinion. Justice Kennedy joined the majority opinion "without reservation." He wrote separately only to emphasize the difficulty he had in deciding to join the majority in this controversial case. Justice Kennedy wrote:

> The hard fact is that sometimes we must make decisions we do not like. We make them because they are right, right in the sense that the law and the Constitution, as we see them, compel the result.

Chief Justice Rehnquist's Dissenting Opinion

Chief Justice William Rehnquist, joined by Justices White and O'Connor, opened his dissent with a detailed history of the American flag. Chief Justice Rehnquist described the first national flag

that the Continental Congress adopted in 1777: It had "thirteen stripes, alternate red and white, [and] thirteen stars, white in a blue field, representing a new constellation." Rehnquist explained: "At the time of the American Revolution, the flag served to unify the Thirteen Colonies at home, while obtaining recognition of national sovereignty abroad."

Chief Justice Rehnquist described the role the flag played in American wars. He told about the flag in the War of 1812 inspiring Francis Scott Key to write "The Star Spangled Banner." Rehnquist noted that the Southern states' rejection of the national flag marked the start of the Civil War. He wrote of the 6,000 Marines who died in hand-to-hand combat in order to raise the American flag over Iwo Jima in World War II. Finally, Rehnquist noted the dire impact flag burnings had on troop morale in Vietnam, which provided the impetus for enacting the Federal Flag Desecration Statute in 1967.

Rehnquist argued:

> The flag is not simply another "idea" or "point of view" competing for recognition in the marketplace of ideas. Millions and millions of Americans regard it with an almost mystical reverence regardless of what sort of social, political, or philosophical beliefs they may have.

Rehnquist turned to the 1942 case of *Chaplinsky v. New Hampshire*. In that case the Supreme Court set out the "fighting words" exception to First Amendment freedom of speech protection. The court said:

> There are certain well-defined and narrowly limited classes of speech, the prevention and punishment of which have never been thought to raise any Constitutional problem. These include the lewd and obscene, the profane, the libelous, and the insulting or "fighting" words—those which by their very utterance inflict injury or tend to incite an immediate breach of the peace.

Rehnquist argued that flag burning, like "fighting words" in *Chaplinsky*, is " 'of such slight social value as a step to truth that any benefit that may be derived from [it] is clearly outweighed' by the public interest in avoiding a probable breach of the peace."

Justice Stevens' Dissenting Opinion

Justice Stevens did not join the main dissent, but instead wrote his own dissenting opinion. Justice Stevens had received the Bronze Star as an officer in the Navy in World War II. He argued that traditional free speech doctrine should not apply to flag burning because of the "intangible dimension" of the flag's deeply symbolic value.

Aftermath of the Decision

The court announced the decision on June 21, 1989, in a rare moment of constitutional drama. Instead of following the customary practice of merely announcing the court's decision, Justice Brennan read much of his opinion aloud. In an even more unusual act, Justice Stevens read his dissenting opinion aloud. The next morning, the *New York Times* reported on the decision as one "virtually certain to be a First Amendment landmark."

Polls found that large majorities of Americans strongly disagreed with the court's ruling. Politicians moved quickly to condemn the decision. President George H.W. Bush, while insisting that he would "fully support" the decision, registered his displeasure with the ruling, calling it "dead wrong." The U.S. Senate, by a margin of 97–3, adopted a resolution expressing "profound disappointment" in the decision. Several Republican members of Congress called for a constitutional amendment to overturn the decision. Many Democrats favored amending the statutory language on flag desecration to comply with a narrow loophole some argued the court had left open.

Eventually Congress passed the Flag Protection Act of 1989. It banned flag burning regardless of whether the person burning the flag intended to cause offense to others. (The Supreme Court had specifically objected to the Texas law because it stressed causing offense.) The new federal law made exceptions for people disposing of a torn or damaged flag. This new law was challenged and reached the Supreme Court next term in *U.S. v. Eichman* (1990). As many had expected, the Supreme Court, with the same justices composing the same 5–4 majority, ruled this statute unconstitutional.

Since 1990, members of Congress have regularly proposed a constitutional amendment to ban flag burning. Such an amendment would require a two-thirds majority in both the House of Representatives and the Senate. Then three-fourths of the state legislatures would have to ratify it. The House has approved such an amendment six times, including, most recently, on June 22, 2005. No proposed amendment, however, has attained the two-thirds majority required in the Senate.

For Discussion

1. As interpreted by the Supreme Court, the right to free speech is not absolute. What are some exceptions to the right to free speech? Do you agree with the exceptions? Explain.

2. What were the facts in *Texas v. Johnson*?

3. Justices Brennan and Stevens and Chief Justice Rehnquist wrote separate opinions and analyzed the case differently. How did each analyze the case? Which opinion do you agree with? Why?

ACTIVITY

The Flag-Burning Amendment

Imagine that you work as aides to a U.S. senator who is on the Judiciary Committee. This committee will be considering the following proposed amendment to the U.S. Constitution:

> The Congress shall have power to prohibit the physical desecration of the flag of the United States.

This amendment would have the effect of overturning the decision in *Texas v. Johnson* and allow Congress to pass legislation against flag burning or other physical acts of disrespect toward the flag.

Your senator has asked for your opinion on this amendment. As a group, do the following:

1. Think of arguments for and against the amendment.

2. Discuss the arguments.

3. Decide whether the senator should support or oppose the amendment.

4. Prepare a presentation to make to the senator, citing reasons for your recommendation.

Bush v. Gore (2000)

The Contested Election of 2000

The 2000 election was one of the closest in U.S. history. Democrat Al Gore won the popular vote, but Republican George W. Bush eventually won the electoral vote.

On December 12, 2000, the U.S. Supreme Court for the first time in American history essentially decided a presidential election with its ruling in *Bush v. Gore*. The day after the Supreme Court's ruling, candidate Al Gore conceded defeat to George W. Bush.

The Events Leading Up to *Bush v. Gore*

The presidential election of Tuesday, November 7, 2000, was one of the closest in U.S. history. By early Wednesday morning, it was clear that the Democratic candidate, Vice President Al Gore, had won the national popular vote, but the outcome of the electoral vote was uncertain. The presidency turned on Florida and its 25 electoral votes. Early on election night, the networks called Gore the winner in Florida, only to retract their prediction later in the evening. In the early hours of Wednesday, November 8, the networks declared Bush the winner of Florida and the presidency, only to recant that a short time later and to conclude that the outcome in Florida, and thus of the national election, was too close to call.

On November 8, the Florida Division of Elections reported that Bush had received 2,909,135 votes and Gore had received 2,907,351 votes. Florida law provides for a recount of votes if the election is decided by less than one-half of a percent of the votes cast. Because the difference in votes between the two candidates was less than one-half of a percent, Gore immediately asked for a machine recount of the tally of votes in four counties: Volusia, Palm Beach, Broward, and Miami-Dade. Florida law set November 14 as the deadline for county vote totals. On November 9, Florida's Secretary of State Katherine Harris declined to extend this deadline. By this point, the machine recount had narrowed Bush's lead to a mere 327 votes.

Upon learning of the close margin between him and Bush, Gore petitioned and received permission to have a hand recount in the four counties in question. On Saturday, November 9, Bush sued in federal district court to block the manual recount, but his request was denied.

Secretary of State Harris, however, declared that November 14 was the deadline for counties to submit their vote totals and that she would not accept late recounts. She said that the Florida election statute required counties to report their votes within one week of the election.

A suit was brought against Harris in Florida court to compel her to accept the time for the reporting of the results. On Friday, November 17, the Florida state trial court ruled in favor of Harris. On Monday, November 20, the Florida Supreme Court held a nationally televised hearing. On Tuesday night, November 21, the Florida Supreme Court unanimously reversed the trial court and ordered that the secretary of state accept hand recounts from the four counties if they were completed by 5 p.m., Sunday, November 26, or Monday morning, if the secretary of state was not open for business on Sunday afternoon.

The Florida Supreme Court ruled that Florida's secretary of state abused her discretion in refusing to extend the deadline for certifying elections to provide the needed time for the recounts. To carry out the law allowing recounts, the court concluded that there must be time for doing the recount. The court said that the secretary of state's refusal to accept hand recounts was wrong because it completely negated the statute that expressly provided for them.

Bush appealed to the U.S. Supreme Court. On Friday, November 24, the day after Thanksgiving, the U.S. Supreme Court granted certiorari and scheduled oral argument for the following Friday, December 1. In an unprecedented order, the court permitted the broadcasting of the oral argument immediately after it was finished. A few days later, in *Bush v. Palm Beach County Canvassing Bd.*, the U.S. Supreme Court sent the case back to the Florida Supreme Court for clarification of its earlier decision.

Meanwhile, on Sunday, November 26, some counties asked for additional time to complete their counting. The secretary of state refused all requests for extensions. On Sunday night, November 26, the Florida Elections Canvassing Commission certified the election results. Bush was determined to be the winner of Florida by 537 votes and thus the winner of Florida's 25 electoral votes.

On Monday, November 27, Gore filed suit in Florida under the Florida law on contesting election results. This provision, Section 102.168(3) (c), provides that "[r]eceipt of a number of illegal votes or rejection of a number of legal votes sufficient to change or place in doubt the result of the election" shall be grounds for a contest. The statute authorizes a court finding successful grounds for a contest to "provide any relief appropriate under such circumstances."

On Saturday and Sunday, December 2 and 3, a Florida state trial court held a hearing on whether Gore had met the statutory requirements for a successful contest. On Monday, December 4, the Florida trial court ruled against Gore on the grounds that Gore failed to prove a "reasonable probability" that the election would have turned out differently if not for problems in counting ballots.

The Florida Supreme Court granted review and scheduled oral arguments for Thursday, December 6. On Friday afternoon, December 7, the Florida Supreme Court, by a 4 to 3 decision,

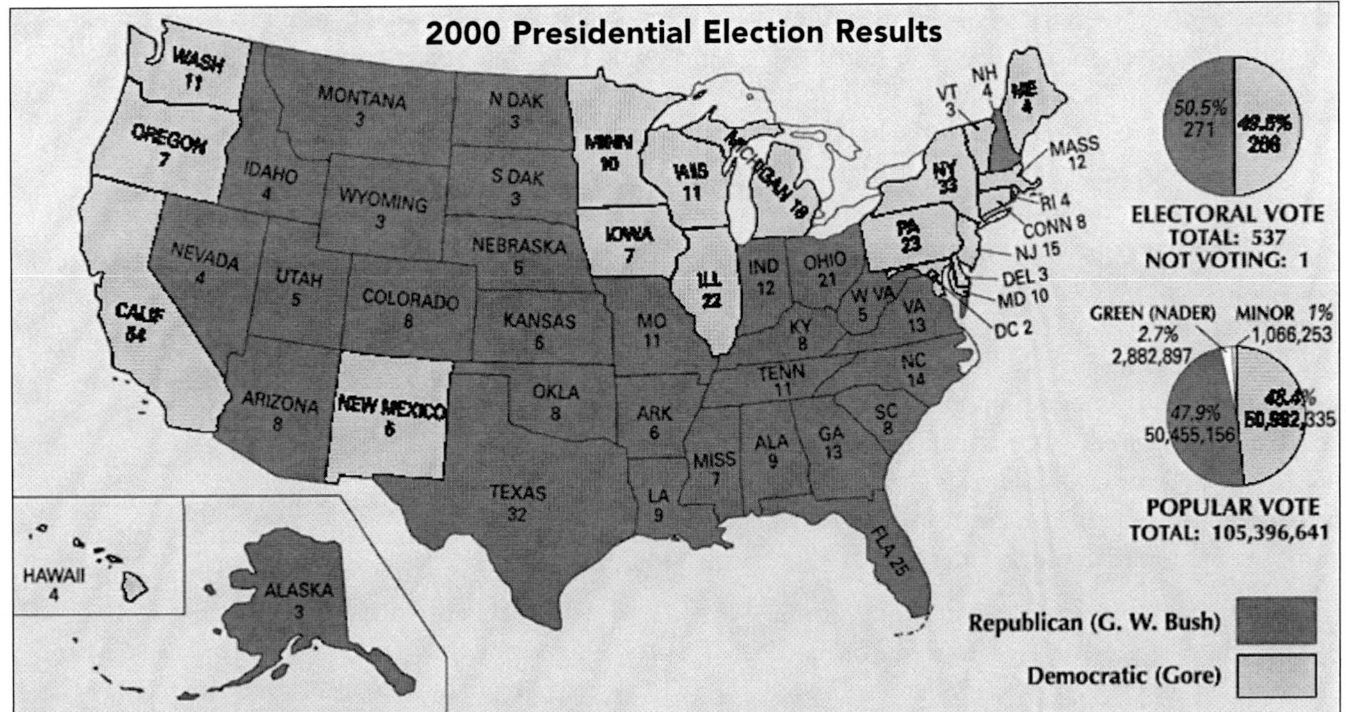

reversed the trial court. The Florida Supreme Court ruled that the trial court had used the wrong standard in insisting that Gore demonstrate a "reasonable probability" that the election would have been decided differently. The Florida Supreme Court said that the statute requires only a showing of "[r]eceipt of a number of illegal votes or rejection of a number of legal votes sufficient to change or place in doubt the result of the election." The Florida Supreme Court ordered a counting of all of the uncounted votes in Florida.

Just hours after the Florida Supreme Court's decision, on Friday night, December 8, a Florida trial court judge ordered that the counting of the uncounted votes commence the next morning and that it be completed by Sunday afternoon, December 9, at 2 p.m. The judge said that he would resolve any disputes.

On Saturday morning, counting commenced as ordered. At the same time, Bush asked the U.S. Supreme Court to stay the counting and grant certiorari in the case. In the early afternoon on Saturday, the U.S. Supreme Court, in a 5 to 4 ruling, halted the counting of the votes in Florida pending its decision.

On Monday, December 11, the U.S. Supreme Court held oral arguments. Again, they were broadcast immediately after their completion. On Tuesday night, December 12, at approximately 10 p.m., Eastern time, the court released its opinion in *Bush v. Gore*.

The Decision

In a per curiam opinion, the Supreme Court ruled 5 to 4 that counting the uncounted ballots without standards denies equal protection and that counting could not continue because Florida wished to choose its electors by the December 12 "safe harbor" date set by federal law. The per curiam opinion was joined by Chief Justice Rehnquist and Justices O'Connor, Scalia, Kennedy, and Thomas.

The court said that the central problem was that the Florida Supreme Court ordered counting the uncounted ballots, but failed to prescribe standards. The per curiam opinion stated: "The problem inheres in absence of specific standards to ensure its equal application. The formulation of uniform rules to determine intent based on these recurring circumstances is practicable and, we conclude, necessary." The court said that this results in similar ballots being treated differently.

Landmarks: Historic U.S. Supreme Court Decisions

The court thus concluded that counting the uncounted ballots as ordered by the Florida Supreme Court would deny equal protection: "The recount process, in its features here described, is inconsistent with the minimum procedures necessary to protect the fundamental right of each voter in the special instance of a statewide recount under the authority of a single state judicial officer." The court explicitly stated that it was deciding just the matter before it and was not setting a general precedent. The per curiam opinion declared: "Our consideration is limited to the present circumstances, for the problem of equal protection in election processes generally presents many complexities."

The court then confronted the key question: Should the case be sent back to the Florida Supreme Court for it to set standards for the counting or should the court order an end to the counting process? The court, in its per curiam opinion, noted that federal law requires the selection of electors to be completed by December 12 and Florida indicated that it wished to observe the December 12 date. The court thus ordered an end to the counting.

Chief Justice Rehnquist wrote a separate opinion concurring in the judgment. Justices Scalia and Thomas joined this opinion. The Rehnquist opinion argued that the Florida Supreme Court had impermissibly changed Florida's election law in a manner that violates federal law. The federal law in question was Section 5 of 3 U.S.C., which provides that the state's selection of electors "shall be conclusive, and shall govern in the counting of the electoral votes" if the electors are chosen under laws enacted prior to election day, and if the selection process is completed six days prior to the meeting of the Electoral College. Chief Justice Rehnquist said that this prevents a state from changing its electoral process after the election and that Florida's Supreme Court had done this by usurping the authority Florida law had vested in the Florida secretary of state and the Florida circuit courts. Chief Justice Rehnquist concluded that the Florida Supreme Court "significantly departed from the statutory framework in place on November 7, and authorized open-ended further proceedings which could not be completed by December 12, thereby preventing a final determination by that date."

The Dissents

Each of the four dissenting justices wrote separate dissents. Justice Stevens, joined by Justices Ginsburg and Breyer, challenged the per curiam's premise that there was a denial of equal protection. He argued that the procedure created by the Florida Supreme Court, with a trial judge resolving disputes, could prevent unequal treatment of like ballots. He explained: "Admittedly, the use of differing substandards for determining voter intent in different counties employing similar voting systems may raise serious concerns. Those concerns are alleviated—if not eliminated—by the fact that a single impartial magistrate will ultimately adjudicate all objections arising from the recount process." Justice Stevens said that if the lack of standard for counting is the problem the solution is to send the case back to Florida to create standards for the subsequent recount.

Justice Souter's dissenting opinion, joined by the other three dissenting justices, objected to the court hearing the case at all. Justice Souter argued that no significant federal issues were raised and that the case should have been left to the Florida courts to resolve.

Justice Ginsburg's dissent argued that there was no denial of equal protection and that in any event, the appropriate solution was to have the case sent back to Florida for the counting to continue.

Finally, Justice Breyer acknowledged that there were equal protection problems with counting votes without standards, but argued that the court was wrong in ending the counting rather than sending back the case for counting with standards. He stressed that the December 12 deadline was not some magic date. States could still choose their electors after that date and could be confident that Congress would recognize them.

Issues to Consider Concerning *Bush v. Gore*

The decision in *Bush v. Gore* raised many issues. One of the most important was whether the court was correct in finding a denial of equal protection. Seven justices expressed concern over a denial of equal protection from counting votes without uniform standards. Yet Justices Souter and Breyer, who shared this concern with the majority, did not file opinions "concurring in part and dissenting in part," but rather just dissented. How, exactly, was equal protection denied?

Another major issue is whether the court has created a new principle of equality in voting. Will this principle be the basis for future successful challenges to variations within a state in election practices? The court stated that it was deciding only the issue before it and not setting a precedent. But its ruling has led to lawsuits across the country arguing that variations within a state in conducting elections violate equal protection.

Finally, another important issue is whether the court was justified in ending the counting in Florida. The court, in its per curiam opinion, said that the Florida Supreme Court had indicated that it wanted to follow the December 12 deadline set by the federal "safe harbor" statute. Since it was December 12, the Supreme Court ordered an end to the counting. But because it was an issue of Florida state law, should the Supreme Court have sent the case back for the Florida Supreme Court to decide the content of Florida law under the unprecedented circumstances?

On December 13, 2000, the day after *Bush v. Gore* was decided, Al Gore conceded the election to George W. Bush. For the first time in history, the Supreme Court had, in effect, decided a presidential election.

For Discussion

1. In the 2000 election, what did the first count of Florida's votes show? On what basis did Al Gore demand a recount? What did the machine recount show?

2. What happened when Gore demanded a manual recount? Do you think a hand recount is more accurate than a machine recount? Explain.

3. A lawsuit was brought to demand an extension of time to report the results of the hand recount. This case ended in a decision by the U.S. Supreme Court on December 1. What decisions were made by the trial court, Florida Supreme Court, and U.S. Supreme Court? Which of these decisions do you think was correct? Why?

4. Gore brought another lawsuit on November 27. What were the grounds for this suit? How did the trial court rule? The Florida Supreme Court? The U.S. Supreme Court? A concurring and four dissenting opinions were also written in *Bush v. Gore*. Which of the opinions—court, concurring, or dissenting—seems most reasonable? Why?

ACTIVITY

Applying *Bush v. Gore*

Although the Supreme Court in its *Bush v. Gore* ruling stated that the case should not be considered as precedent, new cases have arisen challenging election results. None of these cases has reached the Supreme Court. But all of them have cited *Bush v. Gore* as precedent and claimed violations of equal protection. Below are types of cases that have arisen. Imagine that in each case, a statewide election has concluded with extremely close results. The losing candidate in the election is challenging the results citing *Bush v. Gore* and claiming a violation of equal protection.

Your group is the U.S. Supreme Court, and you will decide the case assigned to you. Do the following:

1. Reread and discuss the decision of the court in *Bush v. Gore*.

2. Read your assigned case.

3. Apply the decision in *Bush v. Gore* to your case. Decide whether the case violates the equal protection clause.

4. If you find an equal protection violation, decide on an appropriate remedy for the case. This could be a machine recount, a manual recount, a new election, or some other remedy appropriate for the case.

5. Be prepared to report to the class your decision and your reasons for it.

Cases

State A. In this state, half the voters use modern voting machines, but another half use punch-card machines, which are subject to greater errors. A lawsuit has challenged the election saying that the voters in the half of the state using punch-card machines were denied equal protection.

State B. Provisional ballots are those cast by people who polling officials could not find on the voter lists. State B requires that the voter provide "proper identification." Then the voter can cast a ballot and voting officials later will check to see if that person is indeed entitled to vote. Voters in the state are complaining because officials throughout the state are not accepting the same things as proper identification. A provisional ballot submitted with the same kind of identification might be accepted in one county and rejected in another. A lawsuit has challenged the election, claiming that voters were denied equal protection when their provisional ballots were refused because of "improper identification" when voters in other areas were allowed to cast provisional ballots based on the same type of identification.

State C. Provisional ballots are those cast by people who polling officials could not find on the voter lists. State C has a strict rule that voting officials may accept provisional ballots only if the provisional voter turns in the ballot to the correct precinct. State guidelines require that poll workers instruct provisional voters which precinct to vote in based on their home address. In some polling places, precinct workers ignored these guidelines and failed to notify provisional voters of their proper precinct. As a result, in some precincts, provisional voters were given the proper instructions and in others they were not. A lawsuit has challenged the election, claiming that voters who did not receive the proper instructions were denied equal protection.

State D. This state mandates the use of voting machines. In most of the state, election officials distributed enough machines to most precincts. But in about one-quarter of the state, officials did not distribute enough machines. This resulted in long lines and huge delays discouraging many voters in these precincts from voting. A lawsuit has challenged the election, claiming voters in precincts without sufficient voting machines were denied equal protection.

State E. Provisional ballots are those cast by people who polling officials cannot find on the voter lists. After providing identification, a voter can cast a provisional ballot and voting officials later will check to see if that person is indeed entitled to vote. State E election officials failed to distribute sufficient quantities of provisional ballots. Poll workers in some precincts improvised and allowed provisional voters to fill out blank pieces of paper. In other precincts, poll workers simply informed provisional voters that they could not vote. A lawsuit has challenged the election, arguing that those provisional voters turned away from the polls were denied equal protection.

State F. This state mandates voting machines. In several counties, the election officials decided to distribute the same number of voting machines to each precinct regardless of age, education level, and literacy of the voters in each precinct. Precincts with large numbers of elderly reported long lines and tremendous delays. Many people in these precincts were discouraged from voting. A lawsuit has challenged the election, claiming that the elderly voters in those districts were denied equal protection.

Glossary

acquit (ə KWIT) v. To find not guilty.

adversary system (AD ver sär ē SIS təm) n. Also known as the accusatorial system. In this system of justice, the two opposing parties present evidence. A judge runs the trial but does not investigate the case or otherwise play an active role. *See also* **inquisitorial system.**

affidavit (AF fi dā vit) n. A written statement made under oath.

affirm (ə FERM) v. To uphold the ruling of a lower court.

amicus curiae (ə MĒ kəs KYER ē ī) n. A brief submitted by someone who is not a party to the case. (Latin for "friend of the court.")

appeal (ə PĒL) n. A request that an appellate court review a decision of a lower court.

appellant (ə PEL ənt) n. The party appealing the case. Also know as the **petitioner**. This party's name goes first in the title to the case. Thus, in *Brown v. Board of Education*, Brown was the appellant and the Board of Education was the respondent.

appellate court (ə PEL it KORT) n. A court that hears appeals; not a trial court; an appeals court.

arbitrary (AR bə trär ē) adj. Decided by chance or whim instead of from a principle or rule.

arraignment (ə RĀN ment) n. A court hearing in which the defendant must enter a plea, such as guilty or not guilty.

arrest (ə REST) v. To take a person into custody for the purpose of charging the person with a crime.

associate justice (ə SŌ shē it JUS tis) n. A title for a member of a court who is not the chief justice.

attorney at law *See* **attorney.**

attorney (ə TER nē) n. A lawyer; legal counsel. A person authorized to practice law.

attorney general (ə TER nē JEN er əl) n. 1. The head of the U.S. Department of Justice and member of the president's cabinet. 2. A state's chief law officer, usually a statewide elected position.

bail (BĀL) n. A pretrial procedure permitting an arrested person to stay out of jail by depositing a set amount of money as security that the person will show up for trial.

bench (BENCH) n. 1. The judge's desk in the courtroom. 2. The position of being a judge.

bench trial (BENCH TRĪ əl) n. A trial held before a judge alone without a jury.

bill of attainder (BIL UV ə TĀN der) n. A legislative enactment that punishes a person in place of a trial. Banned by the U.S. Constitution.

Bill of Rights (BIL UV RĪTS) n. The first 10 amendments to the U.S. Constitution, which describe rights and protections guaranteed to each citizen.

brief (BRĒF) 1. n. A written legal argument submitted to a court. 2. n. A summary of an appellate court opinion, typically done by a law student. It summarizes the facts, holding, and reasoning. 3. v. To prepare a written legal argument. 4. v. To summarize an appellate court opinion.

burden of proof (BER dən UV PREWF) n. The responsibility of proving facts in a case. In a criminal trial, the prosecution has the burden of proving its case beyond a reasonable doubt.

burglary (BER glə rē) n. The illegal entry into any building with the intent to commit a crime, such as theft.

capital offense (KAP ə təl ə FENS) n. A crime punishable by death.

capital punishment (CAP ə təl PUN ish mənt) n. The death penalty. A **capital crime** is one that is punishable by death.

case in chief (KĀS IN CHĒF) n. One side's trial evidence. In a criminal trial, the prosecution presents its evidence first. After it rests its case, the defense presents its evidence.

case law (KĀS LO) n. Law made by judges interpreting constitutions, statutes, and other case law; judge-made law.

cause of action (KOZ UV AK shən) n. The facts that give rise to a legal basis to sue.

certworthy (CERT WER *th*ē) adj. A case that raises an issue that merits the court's granting a writ of certiorari.

Pronunciation Key: bat, āte, are, däre, den, ēgo, new, her, bit, īce, î rritate, box, nō, born, oil, book, out, but, ūse, chum, si*ng*, she, thin, *th*e, zh sound in treasure or mirage; ə is the **uh** sound in unaccented syllables.

Landmarks: Historic U.S. Supreme Court Decisions

checks and balances (CHEKS AND BAL əns es) n. A system of government in which the different branches limit each others' powers.

chief justice (CHĒF JUS tis) n. The lead judge in a court with more than one judge. For example, the U.S. Supreme Court has one chief justice and eight associate justices.

civil case (SIV əl KĀS) n. A non-criminal case. Typically, a civil case is a lawsuit between individuals or organizations seeking monetary compensation for damages.

civil court (SIV əl KORT) n. A court that handles civil cases.

clemency (KLEM ən sē) n. 1. Mercy. 2. A pardon.

common law (KOM ən LO) n. 1. The judge-made law in England that evolved over centuries. 2. Judge-made law as opposed to statutory law.

compelling governmental interest (kəm PEL i*ng* GUV ern mənt əl IN trəst) n. An extremely important, vital interest of government.

complaint (kəm PLĀNT) n. In law, a written pleading submitted to a court to begin a lawsuit.

compulsory process (kəm PUL sə rē PROS es) n. A method for obtaining witnesses and evidence for trials. Typically, a person is served with a subpoena ordering the person to appear or produce evidence. Refusal to obey the subpoena can result in charges of contempt of court.

concurring opinion (kən KER i*ng* ə PIN yən) n. A court opinion agreeing with the result in a case, but disagreeing with the reasoning in the court's opinion. Justices writing concurring opinions explain what they believe the reasoning should be.

contempt of court (kən TEMPT UV KORT) n. Showing disrespect for the court or failing to follow a court order. Punishable by a fine or jail time.

covenant (KUV ə nənt) n. A written agreement or contract.

crime (KRĪM) n. An illegal act punishable upon conviction in a court.

defendant (di FEN dənt) n. The accused in a criminal trial or the person being sued in a civil case.

defense attorney (di FENS ə TER nē) n. In a criminal trial, the attorney for the accused. In a civil trial, the attorney for the person being sued.

desecration (DES i krā shən) n. An act of disrespect toward something considered sacred.

discretion (di SKRESH ən) n. The power to choose.

discretionary jurisdiction (di SKRESH ə närē jer əs DIK shən) n. The power of some appeals courts, such as the U.S. Supreme Court, to accept or refuse to hear particular appeals. *See also* **writ of certiorari.**

dissenting opinion (di SENT i*ng* ə PIN yən) n. An opinion by a judge who disagrees with the decision in a case. It explains why the judge disagrees and what the outcome should have been.

double jeopardy (DUB əl JEP er dē) n. Trying a person a second time for a crime that the person has already been acquitted of or been convicted of.

due process (DEW PROS es) n. In the Fifth and 14th amendments, the basic requirement that no person can be deprived of life, liberty, or property without a fair procedures being used. The phrase has also been interpreted to include the fundamental liberties "rooted in the tradition and conscience of our people" (*Palko v. Connecticut*).

en banc (ON BONK) n. The full bench of judges. Each U.S. Appeals Court has from six to 27 judges, but for most cases the judges hear cases in panels of three. When all the judges hear a case together, they hear it *en banc.*

equal protection (ē kwəl prə TEK shən) n. The guarantee that laws will not discriminate against people on the basis of race, religion, skin color, etc. This guarantee is found in the 14th Amendment.

evidence (EV i dəns) n. The means of determining facts in a trial. Testimony, physical objects, and exhibits are examples of evidence.

ex post facto law (EKS POST FAK tō LO) n. A law passed criminalizing an act committed by a person before the law was passed or increasing the penalty for a crime and applying the penalty retroactively. Banned by the U.S. Constitution. (Ex post facto is Latin meaning "from a thing done afterward.")

exclusionary rule (ik SKLEW zhən är ē REWL) n. A judicial rule that prevents the government from introducing illegally obtained evidence at a criminal trial.

executive order (ig ZEK yə tiv OR der) n. A rule or principle issued by the president having the force of law. The authority to issue such an order is based on either a federal law or the constitutional power of the president.

felony (FEL ə nē) n. A serious crime usually punished by one or more years of imprisonment in a state or federal prison.

forfeiture (FOR fi cher) n. The confiscation of assets either used in or derived from illegal activity.

grand jury (GRAND JER ē) n. A group of citizens responsible for determining whether the prosecution has enough evidence against a criminal defendant to justify holding a trial. It meets in secret, and the prosecutor presents evidence to it.

habeas corpus (HĀ bē əs KOR pəs) n. A writ, or court order, for the executive (police, prosecutors, prison officials) to produce a prisoner in court and justify the legality of the imprisonment. (Latin for "you have the body.")

hearing (HÎR i*ng*) n. Any court proceeding, such as a trial.

indict (in DĪT) v. To issue an indictment.

indictment (in DĪT mənt) n. A grand jury's formal charge against a defendant confirming that sufficient evidence exists to justify holding a trial.

indigent (IN di jənt) 1. adj. Unable to afford a lawyer or pay for the expenses of going to court. 2. n. A person unable to afford a lawyer or pay for the expenses of going to court.

in forma pauperis (IN FOR mə PO pə rəs) n. A petition used by the indigent to waive court fees. (Latin meaning "in the form of a pauper.")

injunction (in JUNK shən) n. A court order telling a party to refrain from doing something or to perform a specific action.

inquisitorial system (in KWIZ ə tor ē əl SIS təm) n. A system of justice in which the judges play an active role. They may investigate the case and question witnesses. It is different from an **adversary system** in which the two parties present all the evidence and the judge serves as a referee.

interrogation (IN tär ə gā shən) n. Questioning.

Jim Crow laws (JIM KRŌ LOZ) Laws requiring strict racial segregation. The term "Jim Crow" came from a minstrel show song titled "Jump Jim Crow" in the 1800s. The character "Jim Crow" became a standard in minstrel shows.

judicial review (jew DISH əl rē VŪ) n. The power of the judiciary to review laws and governmental actions to see whether they conform to the Constitution. If they violate the Constitution, the court has the power to overturn them.

jurisdiction (jer əs DIK shən) n. 1. The geographical area over which particular courts have power. 2. The authority to apply the law.

jurisprudence (jer is PREW dəns) n. The philosophy of law, or the science that studies the principles of law.

justice of the peace (JUS tis UV *th*ə PĒS) n. A low-level judge.

justify (JUST ə fī) v. To prove right, good, just, or valid.

lawyer *See* **attorney**.

libel (LĪ bəl) 1. n. Published material that damages a person's reputation. 2. v. To publish libelous material.

lower court (LŌ er KORT) n. 1. A court whose decision is being reviewed by an appeals court. 2. A trial court. 3. A court of limited jurisdiction.

lynching (LINCH i*ng*) n. A form of mob violence that punishes an accused person without a legal trial. The word comes from the American Revolution and a Colonel Charles Lynch of Virginia, who urged crowds to beat and frighten Tories, supporters of Britain.

magistrate (MAJ i strāt) n. A court officer who issues warrants; normally a lower-court judge who handles pretrial proceedings or presides over misdemeanor trials.

majority opinion (mə jor i tē ə pin yən) n. An opinion that a majority of the members of the court agree with.

marshal (MAR shəl) n. A law-enforcement officer who normally performs duties connected with a court.

***Miranda* warning** (mə RAN də WOR ni*ng*) n. A advisory statement about the rights of suspects that police must read to suspects in custody before questioning them. The Supreme Court first required this statement in its *Miranda v. Arizona* decision in 1966.

misdemeanor (mis də MĒ nər) n. A crime less serious than a felony, usually punished by a fine or imprisonment up to one year in a local jail.

motion (MŌ shən) n. A formal request made to a court.

motion to suppress (MŌ shən TEW sə PRES) n. A request that the court exclude particular evidence from the trial because it was illegally obtained.

motive (MŌ təv) n. The reason a person does something.

Pronunciation Key: bat, āte, are, däre, den, ēgo, new, her, bit, īce, îrritate, box, nō, born, oil, book, out, but, ūse, chum, si*ng*, **sh**e, thin, *th*e, **zh** sound in trea**su**re or mira**g**e; ə is the **uh** sound in unaccented syllables.

Landmarks: Historic U.S. Supreme Court Decisions

oral argument (OR əl AR gyə mənt) n. The oral presentation to an appellate court, such as the U.S. Supreme Court, of arguments from both sides in the case. Neither side typically gets to talk without being interrupted by questions from members of the court. The attorneys must be able to think quickly and respond to the questions.

original jurisdiction (ə RIJ e nəl jer əs DIK shən) n. The authority of a court to be the first to hear a case. It is unlike appellate jurisdiction, which authorizes a court to review cases tried by another court.

overrule (ō vər REWL) v. An action by an appellate court, such as the U.S. Supreme Court, to overturn a previous ruling of the court. The overruled case can no longer serve as a precedent.

pardon (PAR dən) 1. n. An official act that forgives all or part of a prisoner's sentence. 2. v. To grant a pardon.

patent law (PA tənt LO) n. The law regarding the protection given to the owners of new inventions. A branch of intellectual property law.

penal (PĒ nəl) adj. Subject to punishment. A **penal code** is a list of laws defining crimes.

penitentiary (pen i TEN shə rē) n. 1. A prison. 2. A state or federal maximum-security prison.

per curiam (PER KYER ē em) n. An unsigned opinion of the court. (Latin meaning "by the court.")

perjure (PER jər) v. To lie under oath; to give false, misleading testimony when one has sworn to tell the truth.

perjury (PER jər ē) n. The crime of lying under oath; giving false, misleading testimony when one has sworn to tell the truth.

petition (pə TISH ən) n. A written request that a court hear an appeal.

petitioner (pə TISH ən er) n. The party appealing the case to a higher court. Also known as the **appellant**.

plaintiff (PLĀN təf) n. The party suing the defendant in a lawsuit.

plead (PLĒD) v. 1. To respond to criminal charges, for example, by answering guilty or not guilty in court. 2. To make or answer formal written allegations to a court.

pleading (PLĒD ing) n. The formal statement, usually written, spelling out the plaintiff's or defendant's case to the court.

plurality opinion (plə RAL i tē ə pin yən) n. An opinion of the court that a majority agrees with the result of the case, but a majority of justices do not agree with the reasoning. For example, in the 2007 U.S. Supreme Court case of *Parents Involved in Community Schools v. Seattle School District*, a majority of five justices agreed that the school district's integration plan was unconstitutional, but only four justices joined the opinion of the court. One other justice (Kennedy) concurred with the result, but not with the reasoning of the court's opinion. Thus the opinion of the court was a plurality, rather than a majority, opinion. Debate arises over whether a plurality opinion can be used as a precedent.

precedent (PRES i dənt) n. An issue of law previously decided by a court that other courts must follow.

probable cause (PROB ə bəl KOZ) n. Evidence that an independent, cautious person would have good reason to believe. The level of proof required for a search warrant.

probate (PRŌ bāt) 1. adj. Concerning wills, trusts, and inheritance. 2. n. The legal process of settling the estate of a person who died either leaving a will or without a will or living trust.

prosecute (PROS ə kūt) v. To try someone for a crime.

prosecution (pros ə KŪ shən) n. The government's side in a criminal case.

prosecutor (PROS ə kū ter) n. The government's attorney who presents the case against a criminal defendant.

public defender (PUB lək də FEND er) n. An attorney working for a government agency (the public defender's office) that defends criminal suspects who cannot afford their own attorney.

public policy (PUB lək POL ə sē) n. A principle, plan, or course of action that a government adopts to address social, economic, or other problems.

quash (KWASH) v. To overturn or set aside (done by a court).

relevant (REL ə vənt) adj. Pertinent, appropriate, related to the subject at hand.

remand (rə MAND) v. To send a case back to a lower court.

respondent (rə SPON dənt) n. The party responding to the appeal. The other party is making the appeal to a higher court. The respondent's name goes last in the title of the case. Thus, in *Brown v. Board of Education*, Brown was the appellant and the Board of Education was the respondent.

reverse (rə VERS) v. To overturn the decision of a lower court.

search (SERCH) v. In *Katz v. U.S.* (1967), the U.S. Supreme Court defined a search as any governmental intrusion into something in which a person has a reasonable expectation of privacy.

search warrant (SERCH WOR ənt) n. An order by a judge authorizing the police to conduct a search.

seizure (SĒ zher) n. Any taking into possession, custody, or control. Property may be seized, but so may people. An arrest is one form of seizure.

self-incrimination (SELF in crim ə NA shən) n. A confession or statements that implicate the person making them in a crime.

sentence (SEN təns) n. The punishment for a crime.

separation of powers (sep ə RĀ shən UV POU ers) n. The division of powers in the U.S. government between the executive, legislative, and judicial branches.

sheriff (SHER əf) n. A county law-enforcement officer.

sovereignty (SOV ər ən tē) n. The authority of an independent state.

special prosecutor (SPESH əl PROS ə kū ter) A lawyer appointed to serve as a prosecutor when there is an apparent conflict of interest between the prosecutor's office and the person under investigation. The special prosecutor is normally a lawyer outside of government.

stare decisis (STÄR ē di SĪ səs) n. The doctrine that courts should follow precedents and its own past decisions. Under this principle, the Supreme Court should not overturn its own decisions unless it has a strong reason to do so. (Latin meaning "stand by past decisions.")

statute (STACH ewt) n. A written law; a law enacted by the legislature.

statutory law *See* **statute**.

subpoena (sə PĒ nə) n. An order to appear in court to testify. (Latin for "under penalty.")

testify (TES tcə fī) v. To make statements as a witness under oath.

testimony (TEST ə mō nē) n. Statements made by witnesses under oath.

tort (TORT) n. A wrongful act (other than breach of contract) that serves as the basis for a lawsuit. The wrongful act usually must be done intentionally or negligently.

tribunal (trī BŪ nəl) n. A court of justice.

vacate (VĀ kāt) v. To annul; to make void.

venue (VEN ū) n. The location of a trial.

verdict (VER dikt) n. In criminal cases, the decision of guilty or not guilty made by the jury or judge. In civil cases, the decision of whether the defendant is liable for damages.

warrant (WOR ənt) n. A court order issued by a judge authorizing police to conduct a search, make an arrest, or a seize evidence of a crime.

writ (RIT) n. A written court order.

writ of certiorari (RIT UV ser shē ə RÄR ē) n. An order from an appeals court, such as the U.S. Supreme Court, stating that the court will hear a case. These writs are granted by appeals courts that have discretionary jurisdiction.

writ of mandamus (RIT UV man DĀ məs) n. A court order telling a government official to take a particular action. (Mandamus is Latin for "we command.")

Pronunciation Key: bat, āte, are, däre, den, ēgo, new, her, bit, īce, îrritate, box, nō, born, oil, book, out, but, ūse, chum, si*ng*, she, thin, *th*e, zh sound in treasure or mirage; ə is the **uh** sound in unaccented syllables.

List of U.S. Supreme Court Justices

#	Judge	Term of Service	Appointed by
110	Samuel Alito	2006–Present	George W. Bush
109	John Glover Roberts, Jr. •	2005–Present	George W. Bush
108	Stephen Breyer	1994–Present	Bill Clinton
107	Ruth Bader Ginsburg	1993–Present	Bill Clinton
106	Clarence Thomas	1991–Present	George H. W. Bush
105	David Souter	1990–Present	George H. W. Bush
104	Anthony Kennedy	1988–Present	Ronald Reagan
103	Antonin Scalia	1986–Present	Ronald Reagan
102	Sandra Day O'Connor	1981–2006	Ronald Reagan
101	John Paul Stevens	1975–Present	Gerald Ford
100	William Hubbs Rehnquist*	1972–2005	Richard Nixon
99	Lewis Franklin Powell, Jr.	1972–1987	Richard Nixon
98	Harry Blackmun	1970–1994	Richard Nixon
97	Warren Earl Burger*	1969–1986	Richard Nixon
96	Thurgood Marshall	1967–1991	Lyndon Johnson
95	Abe Fortas	1965–1969	Lyndon Johnson
94	Arthur Goldberg	1962–1965	John F. Kennedy
93	Byron White	1962–1993	John F. Kennedy
92	Potter Stewart	1958–1981	Dwight D. Eisenhower
91	Charles Evans Whittaker	1957–1962	Dwight D. Eisenhower
90	William J. Brennan	1956–1990	Dwight D. Eisenhower
89	John Marshall Harlan II	1955–1971	Dwight D. Eisenhower
88	Earl Warren*	1953–1969	Dwight D. Eisenhower
87	Sherman Minton	1949–1956	Harry S. Truman
86	Tom C. Clark	1949–1967	Harry S. Truman
85	Fred Moore Vinson*	1946–1953	Harry S. Truman
84	Harold Hitz Burton	1945–1958	Harry S. Truman
83	Wiley Blout Rutledge	1943–1949	Franklin D. Roosevelt
82	Robert H. Jackson	1941–1954	Franklin D. Roosevelt
81	James F. Byrnes	1941–1942	Franklin D. Roosevelt
80	Frank Murphy	1940–1949	Franklin D. Roosevelt
79	William O. Douglas	1939–1975	Franklin D. Roosevelt
78	Felix Frankfurter	1939–1962	Franklin D. Roosevelt
77	Stanley Forman Reed	1938–1957	Franklin D. Roosevelt
76	Hugo Black	1937–1971	Franklin D. Roosevelt
75	Benjamin N. Cardozo	1932–1938	Herbert Hoover
74	Owen Josephus Roberts	1930–1944	Herbert Hoover
73	Harlan Fiske Stone*	1925–1946	Calvin Coolidge
72	Edward Terry Sanford	1923–1930	Warren G. Harding
71	Pierce Butler	1923–1939	Warren G. Harding
70	George Sutherland	1922–1938	Warren G. Harding
69	William Howard Taft*	1921–1930	Warren G. Harding
68	John Hessin Clarke	1916–1922	Woodrow Wilson
67	Louis Brandeis	1916–1939	Woodrow Wilson
66	James Clark McReynolds	1914–1941	Woodrow Wilson
65	Mahlon Pitney	1912–1922	William Howard Taft
64	Joseph Rucker Lamar	1911–1916	William Howard Taft
63	Willis Van Devanter	1911–1937	William Howard Taft
62	Charles Evans Hughes*	1910–1916	William Howard Taft
61	Horace Harmon Lurton	1910–1914	William Howard Taft
60	William Henry Moody	1906–1910	Theodore Roosevelt
59	William R. Day	1903–1922	Theodore Roosevelt
58	Oliver Wendell Holmes, Jr.	1902–1932	Theodore Roosevelt
57	Joseph McKenna	1898–1925	William McKinley

#	Judge	Term of Service	Appointed by
56	Rufus Wheeler Peckham	1896-1909	Grover Cleveland
55	Edward Douglass White*	1894-1921	Grover Cleveland
54	Howell Edmunds Jackson	1893-1895	Benjamin Harrison
53	George Shiras, Jr.	1892-1903	Benjamin Harrison
52	Henry Billings Brown	1891-1906	Benjamin Harrison
51	David Josiah Brewer	1890-1910	Benjamin Harrison
50	Melville Fuller*	1888-1910	Grover Cleveland
49	Lucius Quintus Cincinnatus Lamar	1888-1893	Grover Cleveland
48	Samuel Blatchford	1882-1893	Chester A. Arthur
47	Horace Gray	1882-1902	Chester A. Arthur
46	Thomas Stanley Matthews	1881-1889	James Garfield
45	William Burnham Woods	1881-1887	Rutherford B. Hayes
44	John Marshall Harlan	1877-1911	Rutherford B. Hayes
43	Morrison Remick Waite*	1874-1888	Ulysses S. Grant
42	Ward Hunt	1873-1882	Ulysses S. Grant
41	Joseph Philo Bradley	1870-1892	Ulysses S. Grant
40	William Strong	1870-1880	Ulysses S. Grant
39	Salmon Portland Chase*	1864-1873	Abraham Lincoln
38	Stephen Johnson Field	1863-1897	Abraham Lincoln
37	David Davis	1862-1877	Abraham Lincoln
36	Samuel Freeman Miller	1862-1890	Abraham Lincoln
35	Noah Haynes Swayne	1862-1881	Abraham Lincoln
34	Nathan Clifford	1858-1881	James Buchanan
33	John Archibald Campbell	1853-1861	Franklin Pierce
32	Benjamin Robbins Curtis	1851-1857	Millard Fillmore
31	Robert Cooper Grier	1846-1870	James K. Polk
30	Levi Woodbury	1845-1851	James K. Polk
29	Samuel Nelson	1845-1872	John Tyler
28	Peter Vivian Daniel	1842-1860	Martin Van Buren
27	John McKinley	1838-1852	Martin Van Buren
26	John Catron	1837-1865	Martin Van Buren
25	Philip Pendleton Barbour	1836-1841	Andrew Jackson
24	Roger Brooke Taney*	1836-1864	Andrew Jackson
23	James Moore Wayne	1835-1867	Andrew Jackson
22	Henry Baldwin	1830-1844	Andrew Jackson
21	John McLean	1830-1861	Andrew Jackson
20	Robert Trimble	1826-1828	John Quincy Adams
19	Smith Thompson	1823-1843	James Monroe
18	Joseph Story	1812-1845	James Madison
17	Gabriel Duvall	1811-1835	James Madison
16	Thomas Todd	1807-1826	Thomas Jefferson
15	Henry Brockholst Livingston	1807-1823	Thomas Jefferson
14	William Johnson	1804-1834	Thomas Jefferson
13	John Marshall*	1801-1835	John Adams
12	Alfred Moore	1800-1804	John Adams
11	Bushrod Washington	1799-1829	John Adams
10	Oliver Ellsworth*	1796-1800	George Washington
9	Samuel Chase	1796-1811	George Washington
8	William Paterson	1793-1806	George Washington
7	Thomas Johnson	1792-1793	George Washington
6	James Iredell	1790-1799	George Washington
5	John Rutledge*	1790-1791, 1795	George Washington
4	John Blair	1790-1795	George Washington
3	William Cushing*	1790-1810	George Washington
2	John Jay*	1789-1795	George Washington
1	James Wilson	1789-1798	George Washington

*Denotes a chief justice at some point in time.

List of Chief Justices of the U.S. Supreme Court

#	Chief Justice	Term of Service as Chief Justice	Appointed by
17	John Glover Roberts Jr.	2005–Present	George W. Bush
16	William Hubbs Rehnquist	1986–2005	Ronald Reagan
15	Warren Earl Burger	1969–1986	Richard Nixon
14	Earl Warren	1953–1969	Dwight D. Eisenhower
13	Frederick Moore Vinson	1946–1953	Harry S. Truman
12	Harlan Fiske Stone	1941–1946	Franklin D. Roosevelt
11	Charles Evans Hughes	1930–1941	Herbert Hoover
10	William Howard Taft	1921–1930	Warren G. Harding
9	Edward Douglass White	1910–1921	William Howard Taft
8	Melville Weston Fuller	1888–1910	Grover Cleveland
7	Morrison Remick Waite	1874–1888	Ulysses S. Grant
6	Salman Portland Chase	1864–1873	Abraham Lincoln
5	Roger Brooke Taney	1836–1864	Andrew Jackson
4	John Marshall	1801–1835	John Adams
3	Oliver Ellsworth	1796–1800	George Washington
2	John Rutledge	1795–1795	George Washington
1	John Jay	1789–1795	George Washington

U.S. Constitution

Preamble

We the People of the United States, in Order to form a more perfect Union, establish Justice, insure domestic Tranquility, provide for the common defence, promote the general Welfare, and secure the Blessings of Liberty to ourselves and our Posterity, do ordain and establish this Constitution for the United States of America.

Article I

Section 1

All legislative Powers herein granted shall be vested in a Congress of the United States, which shall consist of a Senate and House of Representatives.

Section 2

[Clause 1] The House of Representatives shall be composed of Members chosen every second Year by the People of the several States, and the Electors in each State shall have the Qualifications requisite for Electors of the most numerous Branch of the State Legislature.

[Clause 2] No Person shall be a Representative who shall not have attained to the Age of twenty five Years, and been seven Years a Citizen of the United States, and who shall not, when elected, be an Inhabitant of that State in which he shall be chosen.

[Clause 3] Representatives and direct Taxes shall be apportioned among the several States which may be included within this Union, according to their respective Numbers, which shall be determined by adding to the whole Number of free Persons, including those bound to Service for a Term of Years, and excluding Indians not taxed, three fifths of all other Persons. The actual Enumeration shall be made within three Years after the first Meeting of the Congress of the United States, and within every subsequent Term of ten Years, in such Manner as they shall by Law direct. The Number of Representatives shall not exceed one for every thirty Thousand, but each State shall have at Least one Representative; and until such enumeration shall be made, the State of New Hampshire shall be entitled to chuse three, Massachusetts eight, Rhode-Island and Providence Plantations one, Connecticut five, New-York six, New Jersey four, Pennsylvania eight, Delaware one, Maryland six, Virginia ten, North Carolina five, South Carolina five, and Georgia three.

[Clause 4] When vacancies happen in the Representation from any State, the Executive Authority thereof shall issue Writs of Election to fill such Vacancies.

[Clause 5] The House of Representatives shall chuse their Speaker and other Officers; and shall have the sole Power of Impeachment.

Section 3

[Clause 1] The Senate of the United States shall be composed of two Senators from each State, chosen by the Legislature thereof, for six Years; and each Senator shall have one Vote.

[Clause 2] Immediately after they shall be assembled in Consequence of the first Election, they shall be divided as equally as may be into three Classes. The Seats of the Senators of the first Class shall be vacated at the Expiration of the second Year, of the second Class at the Expiration of the fourth Year, and of the third Class at the Expiration of the sixth Year, so that one third may be chosen every second Year; and if Vacancies happen by Resignation, or otherwise, during the Recess of the Legislature of any State, the Executive thereof may make temporary Appointments until the next Meeting of the Legislature, which shall then fill such Vacancies.

[Clause 3] No Person shall be a Senator who shall not have attained to the Age of thirty Years, and been nine Years a Citizen of the United States, and who shall not, when elected, be an Inhabitant of that State for which he shall be chosen.

[Clause 4] The Vice President of the United States shall be President of the Senate, but shall have no Vote, unless they be equally divided.

[Clause 5] The Senate shall chuse their other Officers, and also a President pro tempore, in the Absence of the Vice President, or when he shall exercise the Office of President of the United States.

[Clause 6] The Senate shall have the sole Power to try all Impeachments. When sitting for that Purpose, they shall be on Oath or Affirmation. When the President of the United States is tried, the Chief Justice shall preside: And no Person shall be convicted without the Concurrence of two thirds of the Members present.

[Clause 7] Judgment in Cases of Impeachment shall not extend further than to removal from Office, and disqualification to hold and enjoy any Office of honor, Trust or Profit under the United States: but the Party convicted shall nevertheless be liable and subject to Indictment, Trial, Judgment and Punishment, according to Law.

Section 4

[Clause 1] The Times, Places and Manner of holding Elections for Senators and Representatives, shall be prescribed in each State by the Legislature thereof; but the Congress may at any time by Law make or alter such Regulations, except as to the Places of chusing Senators.

[Clause 2] The Congress shall assemble at least once in every Year, and such Meeting shall be on the first Monday in December, unless they shall by Law appoint a different Day.

Section 5

[Clause 1] Each House shall be the Judge of the Elections, Returns and Qualifications of its own Members, and a Majority of each shall constitute a Quorum to do Business; but a smaller Number may adjourn from day to day, and may be authorized to compel the Attendance of absent Members, in such Manner, and under such Penalties as each House may provide.

[Clause 2] Each House may determine the Rules of its Proceedings, punish its Members for disorderly Behaviour, and, with the Concurrence of two thirds, expel a Member.

[Clause 3] Each House shall keep a Journal of its Proceedings, and from time to time publish the same, excepting such Parts as may in their Judgment require Secrecy; and the Yeas and Nays of the Members of either House on any question shall, at the Desire of one fifth of those Present, be entered on the Journal.

[Clause 4] Neither House, during the Session of Congress, shall, without the Consent of the other, adjourn for more than three days, nor to any other Place than that in which the two Houses shall be sitting.

Section 6

[Clause 1] The Senators and Representatives shall receive a Compensation for their Services, to be ascertained by Law, and paid out of the Treasury of the United States. They shall in all Cases, except Treason, Felony and Breach of the Peace, be privileged from Arrest during their Attendance at the Session of their respective Houses, and in going to and returning from the same; and for any Speech or Debate in either House, they shall not be questioned in any other Place.

[Clause 2] No Senator or Representative shall, during the Time for which he was elected, be appointed to any civil Office under the Authority of the United States, which shall have been created, or the Emoluments whereof shall have been encreased during such time; and no Person holding any Office under the United States, shall be a Member of either House during his Continuance in Office.

Section 7

[Clause 1] All Bills for raising Revenue shall originate in the House of Representatives; but the Senate may propose or concur with Amendments as on other Bills.

[Clause 2] Every Bill which shall have passed the House of Representatives and the Senate, shall, before it become a Law, be presented to the President of the United States; If he approve he shall sign it, but if not he shall return it, with his Objections to that House in which it shall have originated, who shall enter the Objections at large on their Journal, and proceed to reconsider it. If after such Reconsideration two thirds of that House shall agree to pass the Bill, it shall be sent, together with the Objections, to the other House, by which it shall likewise be reconsidered, and if approved by two thirds of that House, it shall become a Law. But in all such Cases the Votes of both Houses shall be determined by yeas and Nays, and the Names of the Persons voting for and against the Bill shall be entered on the Journal of each House respectively. If any Bill shall not be returned by the President within ten Days (Sundays excepted) after it shall have been presented to him, the Same shall be a Law, in like Manner as if he had signed it, unless the Congress by their Adjournment prevent its Return, in which Case it shall not be a Law.

[Clause 3] Every Order, Resolution, or Vote to which the Concurrence of the Senate and House of Representatives may be necessary (except on a question of Adjournment) shall be presented to the President of the United States; and before the Same shall take Effect, shall be approved by him, or being disapproved by him, shall be repassed by two thirds of the Senate and House of Representatives, according to the Rules and Limitations prescribed in the Case of a Bill.

Section 8

[Clause 1] The Congress shall have Power To lay and collect Taxes, Duties, Imposts and Excises, to pay the Debts and provide for the common Defence and general Welfare of the United States; but all Duties, Imposts and Excises shall be uniform throughout the United States;

[Clause 2] To borrow Money on the credit of the United States;

[Clause 3] To regulate Commerce with foreign Nations, and among the several States, and with the Indian Tribes;

[Clause 4] To establish an uniform Rule of Naturalization, and uniform Laws on the subject of Bankruptcies throughout the United States;

[Clause 5] To coin Money, regulate the Value thereof, and of foreign Coin, and fix the Standard of Weights and Measures;

[Clause 6] To provide for the Punishment of counterfeiting the Securities and current Coin of the United States;

[Clause 7] To establish Post Offices and post Roads;

[Clause 8] To promote the Progress of Science and useful Arts, by securing for limited Times to Authors and Inventors the exclusive Right to their respective Writings and Discoveries;

[Clause 9] To constitute Tribunals inferior to the supreme Court;

[Clause 10] To define and punish Piracies and Felonies committed on the high Seas, and Offences against the Law of Nations;

[Clause 11] To declare War, grant Letters of Marque and Reprisal, and make Rules concerning Captures on Land and Water;

[Clause 12] To raise and support Armies, but no Appropriation of Money to that Use shall be for a longer Term than two Years;

[Clause 13] To provide and maintain a Navy;

[Clause 14] To make Rules for the Government and Regulation of the land and naval Forces;

[Clause 15] To provide for calling forth the Militia to execute the Laws of the Union, suppress Insurrections and repel Invasions;

[Clause 16] To provide for organizing, arming, and disciplining, the Militia, and for governing such Part of them as may be employed in the Service of the United States, reserving to the States respectively, the Appointment of the Officers, and the Authority of training the Militia according to the discipline prescribed by Congress;

[Clause 17] To exercise exclusive Legislation in all Cases whatsoever, over such District (not exceeding ten Miles square) as may, by Cession of particular States, and the Acceptance of Congress, become the Seat of the Government of the United States, and to exercise like Authority over all Places purchased by the Consent of the Legislature of the State in which the Same shall be, for the Erection of Forts, Magazines, Arsenals, dock-Yards, and other needful Buildings;—And

[Clause 18] To make all Laws which shall be necessary and proper for carrying into Execution the foregoing Powers, and all other Powers vested by this Constitution in the Government of the United States, or in any Department or Officer thereof.

Section 9

[Clause 1] The Migration or Importation of such Persons as any of the States now existing shall think proper to admit, shall not be prohibited by the Congress prior to the Year one thousand eight hundred and eight, but a Tax or duty may be imposed on such Importation, not exceeding ten dollars for each Person.

[Clause 2] The Privilege of the Writ of Habeas Corpus shall not be suspended, unless when in Cases of Rebellion or Invasion the public Safety may require it.

[Clause 3] No Bill of Attainder or ex post facto Law shall be passed.

[Clause 4] No Capitation, or other direct, Tax shall be laid, unless in Proportion to the Census or Enumeration herein before directed to be taken.

[Clause 5] No Tax or Duty shall be laid on Articles exported from any State.

[Clause 6] No Preference shall be given by any Regulation of Commerce or Revenue to the Ports of one State over those of another: nor shall Vessels bound to, or from, one State, be obliged to enter, clear, or pay Duties in another.

[Clause 7] No Money shall be drawn from the Treasury, but in Consequence of Appropriations made by Law; and a regular Statement and Account of the Receipts and Expenditures of all public Money shall be published from time to time.

[Clause 8] No Title of Nobility shall be granted by the United States: And no Person holding any Office of Profit or Trust under them, shall, without the Consent of the Congress, accept of any present, Emolument, Office, or Title, of any kind whatever, from any King, Prince, or foreign State.

Section 10

[Clause 1] No State shall enter into any Treaty, Alliance, or Confederation; grant Letters of Marque and Reprisal; coin Money; emit Bills of Credit; make any Thing but gold and silver Coin a Tender in Payment of Debts; pass any Bill of Attainder, ex post facto Law, or Law impairing the Obligation of Contracts, or grant any Title of Nobility.

[Clause 2] No State shall, without the Consent of the Congress, lay any Imposts or Duties on Imports or Exports, except what may be absolutely necessary for executing it's inspection Laws: and the net Produce of all Duties and Imposts, laid by any State on Imports or Exports, shall be for the Use of the Treasury of the United States; and all such Laws shall be subject to the Revision and Controul of the Congress.

[Clause 3] No State shall, without the Consent of Congress, lay any Duty of Tonnage, keep Troops, or Ships of War in time of Peace, enter into any Agreement or Compact with another State, or with a foreign Power, or engage in War, unless actually invaded, or in such imminent Danger as will not admit of delay.

Article II

Section 1

[Clause 1] The executive Power shall be vested in a President of the United States of America. He shall hold his Office during the Term of four Years, and, together with the Vice President, chosen for the same Term, be elected, as follows

[Clause 2] Each State shall appoint, in such Manner as the Legislature thereof may direct, a Number of Electors, equal to the whole Number of Senators and Representatives to which the State may be entitled in the Congress: but no Senator or Representative, or Person holding an Office of Trust or Profit under the United States, shall be appointed an Elector.

[Clause 3] The Electors shall meet in their respective States, and vote by Ballot for two Persons, of whom one at least shall not be an Inhabitant of the same State with themselves. And they shall make a List of all the Persons voted for, and of the Number of Votes for each; which List they shall sign and certify, and transmit sealed to the Seat of the Government of the United States, directed to the President of the Senate. The President of the Senate shall, in the Presence of the Senate and House of Representatives, open all the Certificates, and the Votes shall then be counted. The Person having the greatest Number of Votes shall be the President, if such Number be a Majority of the whole Number of Electors appointed; and if there be more than one who have such Majority, and have an equal Number of Votes, then the House of Representatives shall immediately chuse by Ballot one of them for President; and if no Person have a Majority, then from the five highest on the List the said House shall in like Manner chuse the President. But in chusing the President, the Votes shall be taken by States, the Representation from each State having one Vote; A quorum for this Purpose shall consist of a Member or Members from two thirds of the States, and a Majority of all the States shall be necessary to a Choice. In every Case, after the Choice of the President, the Person having the greatest Number of Votes of the Electors shall be the Vice President. But if there should remain two or more who have equal Votes, the Senate shall chuse from them by Ballot the Vice President.

[Clause 4] The Congress may determine the Time of chusing the Electors, and the Day on which they shall give their Votes; which Day shall be the same throughout the United States.

[Clause 5] No Person except a natural born Citizen, or a Citizen of the United States, at the time of the Adoption of this Constitution, shall be eligible to the Office of President; neither shall any Person be eligible to that Office who shall not have attained to the Age of thirty five Years, and been fourteen Years a Resident within the United States.

[Clause 6] In Case of the Removal of the President from Office, or of his Death, Resignation, or Inability to discharge the Powers and Duties of the said Office, the Same shall devolve on the Vice President, and the Congress may by Law provide for the Case of Removal, Death, Resignation or Inability, both of the President and Vice President, declaring what Officer shall then act as President, and such Officer shall act accordingly, until the Disability be removed, or a President shall be elected.

[Clause 7] The President shall, at stated Times, receive for his Services, a Compensation, which shall neither be encreased nor diminished during the Period for which he shall have been elected, and he shall not receive within that Period any other Emolument from the United States, or any of them.

[Clause 8] Before he enter on the Execution of his Office, he shall take the following Oath or Affirmation:—"I do solemnly swear (or affirm) that I will faithfully execute the Office of President of the United States, and will to the best of my Ability, preserve, protect and defend the Constitution of the United States."

Section 2

[Clause 1] The President shall be Commander in Chief of the Army and Navy of the United States, and of the Militia of the several States, when called into the actual Service of the United States; he may require the Opinion, in writing, of the principal Officer in each of the executive Departments, upon any Subject relating to the Duties of their respective Offices, and he shall have Power to grant Reprieves and Pardons for Offences against the United States, except in Cases of Impeachment.

[Clause 2] He shall have Power, by and with the Advice and Consent of the Senate, to make Treaties, provided two thirds of the Senators present concur; and he shall nominate, and by and with the Advice and Consent of the Senate, shall appoint Ambassadors, other public Ministers and Consuls, Judges of the supreme Court, and all other Officers of the United States, whose Appointments are not herein otherwise provided for, and which shall be established by Law: but the Congress may by Law vest the Appointment of such inferior Officers, as they think proper, in the President alone, in the Courts of Law, or in the Heads of Departments.

[Clause 3] The President shall have Power to fill up all Vacancies that may happen during the Recess of the Senate, by granting Commissions which shall expire at the End of their next Session.

Section 3

He shall from time to time give to the Congress Information of the State of the Union, and recommend to their Consideration such Measures as he shall judge necessary and expedient; he may, on extraordinary Occasions, convene both Houses, or either of them, and in Case of Disagreement between them, with Respect to the Time of Adjournment, he may adjourn them to such Time as he shall think proper; he shall receive Ambassadors and other public Ministers; he shall take Care that the Laws be faithfully executed, and shall Commission all the Officers of the United States.

Section 4

The President, Vice President and all civil Officers of the United States, shall be removed from Office on Impeachment for, and Conviction of, Treason, Bribery, or other high Crimes and Misdemeanors.

Article III

Section 1

The judicial Power of the United States, shall be vested in one supreme Court, and in such inferior Courts as the Congress may from time to time ordain and establish. The Judges, both of the supreme and inferior Courts, shall hold their Offices during good Behaviour, and shall, at stated Times, receive for their Services, a Compensation, which shall not be diminished during their Continuance in Office.

Section 2

[Clause 1] The judicial Power shall extend to all Cases, in Law and Equity, arising under this Constitution, the Laws of the United States, and Treaties made, or which shall be made, under their Authority;—to all Cases affecting Ambassadors, other public Ministers and Consuls;—to all Cases of admiralty and maritime Jurisdiction;—to Controversies to which the United States shall be a Party;—to Controversies between two or more States;—between a State and Citizens of another State;—between Citizens of different States, —between Citizens of the same State claiming Lands under Grants of different States, and between a State, or the Citizens thereof, and foreign States, Citizens or Subjects.

[Clause 2] In all Cases affecting Ambassadors, other public Ministers and Consuls, and those in which a State shall be Party, the supreme Court shall have original Jurisdiction. In all the other Cases before mentioned, the supreme Court shall have appellate Jurisdiction, both as to Law and Fact, with such Exceptions, and under such Regulations as the Congress shall make.

[Clause 3] The Trial of all Crimes, except in Cases of Impeachment, shall be by Jury; and such Trial shall be held in the State where the said Crimes shall have been committed; but when not committed within any State, the Trial shall be at such Place or Places as the Congress may by Law have directed.

Section 3

[Clause 1] Treason against the United States, shall consist only in levying War against them, or in adhering to their Enemies, giving them Aid and Comfort. No Person shall be convicted of Treason unless on the Testimony of two

Witnesses to the same overt Act, or on Confession in open Court.

[Clause 2] The Congress shall have Power to declare the Punishment of Treason, but no Attainder of Treason shall work Corruption of Blood, or Forfeiture except during the Life of the Person attainted.

Article IV

Section 1

Full Faith and Credit shall be given in each State to the public Acts, Records, and judicial Proceedings of every other State. And the Congress may by general Laws prescribe the Manner in which such Acts, Records and Proceedings shall be proved, and the Effect thereof.

Section 2

[Clause 1] The Citizens of each State shall be entitled to all Privileges and Immunities of Citizens in the several States.

[Clause 2] A Person charged in any State with Treason, Felony, or other Crime, who shall flee from Justice, and be found in another State, shall on Demand of the executive Authority of the State from which he fled, be delivered up, to be removed to the State having Jurisdiction of the Crime.

[Clause 3] No Person held to Service or Labour in one State, under the Laws thereof, escaping into another, shall, in Consequence of any Law or Regulation therein, be discharged from such Service or Labour, but shall be delivered up on Claim of the Party to whom such Service or Labour may be due.

Section 3

[Clause 1] New States may be admitted by the Congress into this Union; but no new State shall be formed or erected within the Jurisdiction of any other State; nor any State be formed by the Junction of two or more States, or Parts of States, without the Consent of the Legislatures of the States concerned as well as of the Congress.

[Clause 2] The Congress shall have Power to dispose of and make all needful Rules and Regulations respecting the Territory or other Property belonging to the United States; and nothing in this Constitution shall be so construed as to Prejudice any Claims of the United States, or of any particular State.

Section 4

The United States shall guarantee to every State in this Union a Republican Form of Government, and shall protect each of them against Invasion; and on Application of the Legislature, or of the Executive (when the Legislature cannot be convened) against domestic Violence.

Article V

The Congress, whenever two thirds of both Houses shall deem it necessary, shall propose Amendments to this Constitution, or, on the Application of the Legislatures of two thirds of the several States, shall call a Convention for proposing Amendments, which, in either Case, shall be valid to all Intents and Purposes, as Part of this Constitution, when ratified by the Legislatures of three fourths of the several States, or by Conventions in three fourths thereof, as the one or the other Mode of Ratification may be proposed by the Congress; Provided that no Amendment which may be made prior to the Year One thousand eight hundred and eight shall in any Manner affect the first and fourth Clauses in the Ninth Section of the first Article; and that no State, without its Consent, shall be deprived of its equal Suffrage in the Senate.

Article VI

[Clause 1] All Debts contracted and Engagements entered into, before the Adoption of this Constitution, shall be as valid against the United States under this Constitution, as under the Confederation.

[Clause 2] This Constitution, and the Laws of the United States which shall be made in Pursuance thereof; and all Treaties made, or which shall be made, under the Authority of the United States, shall be the supreme Law of the Land; and the Judges in every State shall be bound thereby, any Thing in the Constitution or Laws of any State to the Contrary notwithstanding.

[Clause 3] The Senators and Representatives before mentioned, and the Members of the several State Legislatures, and all executive and judicial Officers, both of the United States and of the several States, shall be bound by Oath or Affirmation, to support this Constitution; but no religious Test shall ever be required as a Qualification to any Office or public Trust under the United States.

Article VII

The Ratification of the Conventions of nine States, shall be sufficient for the Establishment of this Constitution between the States so ratifying the Same.

Done in Convention by the Unanimous Consent of the States present the Seventeenth Day of September in the Year of our Lord one thousand seven hundred and Eighty seven and of the Independence of the United States of America the Twelfth In witness whereof We have hereunto subscribed our Names,

Signers

George Washington, President and deputy from Virginia

Connecticut: William S. Johnson, Roger Sherman

Delaware: George Read, Gunning Bedford Jr., John Dickinson, Richard Bassett, Jacob Broom

Georgia: William Few, Abraham Baldwin

Maryland: James McHenry, Daniel of St Thomas Jenifer, Daniel Carroll

Massachusetts: Nathaniel Gorham, Rufus King

New Hampshire: John Langdon, Nicholas Gilman

New York: Alexander Hamilton

New Jersey: William Livingston, David Brearly, William Paterson, Jonathan Dayton

North Carolina: William Blount, Richard Dobbs Spaight, Hu Williamson

Pennsylvania: Benjamin Franklin, Thomas Mifflin, Robert Morris, George Clymer, Thomas Fitzsimons, Jared Ingersoll, James Wilson, Gouverneur Morris

South Carolina: J. Rutledge, Charles C. Pinckney, Charles Pinckney, Pierce Butler

Virginia: John Blair, James Madison Jr.

Amendments

[The Bill of Rights. These are the first 10 amendments to the Constitution. They were ratified in 1791.]

Amendment I

Congress shall make no law respecting an establishment of religion, or prohibiting the free exercise thereof; or abridging the freedom of speech, or of the press; or the right of the people peaceably to assemble, and to petition the Government for a redress of grievances.

Amendment II

A well regulated Militia, being necessary to the security of a free State, the right of the people to keep and bear Arms, shall not be infringed.

Amendment III

No Soldier shall, in time of peace be quartered in any house, without the consent of the Owner, nor in time of war, but in a manner to be prescribed by law.

Amendment IV

The right of the people to be secure in their persons, houses, papers, and effects, against unreasonable searches and seizures, shall not be violated, and no Warrants shall issue, but upon probable cause, supported by Oath or affirmation, and particularly describing the place to be searched, and the persons or things to be seized.

Amendment V

No person shall be held to answer for a capital, or otherwise infamous crime, unless on a presentment or indictment of a Grand Jury, except in cases arising in the land or naval forces, or in the Militia, when in actual service in time of War or public danger; nor shall any person be subject for the same offence to be twice put in jeopardy of life or limb; nor shall be compelled in any criminal case to be a witness against himself, nor be deprived of life, liberty, or property, without due process of law; nor shall private property be taken for public use, without just compensation.

Amendment VI

In all criminal prosecutions, the accused shall enjoy the right to a speedy and public trial, by an impartial jury of the State and district wherein the crime shall have been committed, which district shall have been previously ascertained by law, and to be informed of the nature and cause of the accusation; to be confronted with the witnesses against him; to have compulsory process for obtaining witnesses in his favor, and to have the Assistance of Counsel for his defence.

Amendment VII

In Suits at common law, where the value in controversy shall exceed twenty dollars, the right of trial by jury shall be preserved, and no fact tried by a jury, shall be otherwise re-examined in any Court of the United States, than according to the rules of the common law.

Amendment VIII

Excessive bail shall not be required, nor excessive fines imposed, nor cruel and unusual punishments inflicted.

Amendment IX

The enumeration in the Constitution, of certain rights, shall not be construed to deny or disparage others retained by the people.

Amendment X

The powers not delegated to the United States by the Constitution, nor prohibited by it to the States, are reserved to the States respectively, or to the people.

[Later Amendments]

Amendment XI [1798]

The Judicial power of the United States shall not be construed to extend to any suit in law or equity, commenced or prosecuted against one of the United States by Citizens of another State, or by Citizens or Subjects of any Foreign State.

Amendment XII [1804]

The Electors shall meet in their respective states, and vote by ballot for President and Vice-President, one of whom, at least, shall not be an inhabitant of the same state with themselves; they shall name in their ballots the person voted for as President, and in distinct ballots the person voted for as Vice-President, and they shall make distinct lists of all persons voted for as President, and of all persons voted for as Vice-President, and of the number of votes for each, which lists they shall sign and certify, and transmit sealed to the seat of the government of the United States, directed to the President of the Senate;—The President of the Senate shall, in the presence of the Senate and House of Representatives, open all the certificates and the votes shall then be counted;—The person having the greatest number of votes for President, shall be the President, if such number be a majority of the whole number of Electors appointed; and if no person have such majority, then from the persons having the highest numbers not exceeding three on the list of those voted for as President, the House of Representatives shall choose immediately, by ballot, the President. But in choosing the President, the votes shall be taken by states, the representation from each state having one vote; a quorum for this purpose shall consist of a member or members from two-thirds of the states, and a majority of all the states shall be necessary to a choice. And if the House of Representatives shall not choose a President whenever the right of choice shall devolve upon them, before the fourth day of March next following, then the

Vice-President shall act as President, as in the case of the death or other constitutional disability of the President.

The person having the greatest number of votes as Vice-President, shall be the Vice-President, if such number be a majority of the whole number of Electors appointed, and if no person have a majority, then from the two highest numbers on the list, the Senate shall choose the Vice-President; a quorum for the purpose shall consist of two-thirds of the whole number of Senators, and a majority of the whole number shall be necessary to a choice. But no person constitutionally ineligible to the office of President shall be eligible to that of Vice-President of the United States.

Amendment XIII [1865]

Section 1. Neither slavery nor involuntary servitude, except as a punishment for crime whereof the party shall have been duly convicted, shall exist within the United States, or any place subject to their jurisdiction.

Section 2. Congress shall have power to enforce this article by appropriate legislation.

Amendment XIV [1868]

Section 1. All persons born or naturalized in the United States, and subject to the jurisdiction thereof, are citizens of the United States and of the State wherein they reside. No State shall make or enforce any law which shall abridge the privileges or immunities of citizens of the United States; nor shall any State deprive any person of life, liberty, or property, without due process of law; nor deny to any person within its jurisdiction the equal protection of the laws.

Section 2. Representatives shall be apportioned among the several States according to their respective numbers, counting the whole number of persons in each State, excluding Indians not taxed. But when the right to vote at any election for the choice of electors for President and Vice President of the United States, Representatives in Congress, the Executive and Judicial officers of a State, or the members of the Legislature thereof, is denied to any of the male inhabitants of such State, being twenty-one years of age, and citizens of the United States, or in any way abridged, except for participation in rebellion, or other crime, the basis of representation therein shall be reduced in the proportion which the number of such male citizens shall bear to the whole number of male citizens twenty-one years of age in such State.

Section 3. No person shall be a Senator or Representative in Congress, or elector of President and Vice President, or hold any office, civil or military, under the United States, or under any State, who, having previously taken an oath, as a member of Congress, or as an officer of the United States, or as a member of any State legislature, or as an executive or judicial officer of any State, to support the Constitution of the United States, shall have engaged in insurrection or rebellion against the same, or given aid or comfort to the enemies thereof. But Congress may by a vote of two-thirds of each House, remove such disability.

Section 4. The validity of the public debt of the United States, authorized by law, including debts incurred for payment of pensions and bounties for services in suppressing insurrection or rebellion, shall not be questioned. But neither the United States nor any State shall assume or pay any debt or obligation incurred in aid of insurrection or rebellion against the United States, or any claim for the loss or emancipation of any slave; but all such debts, obligations and claims shall be held illegal and void.

Section 5. The Congress shall have power to enforce, by appropriate legislation, the provisions of this article.

Amendment XV [1870]

Section 1. The right of citizens of the United States to vote shall not be denied or abridged by the United States or by any State on account of race, color, or previous condition of servitude.

Section 2. The Congress shall have power to enforce this article by appropriate legislation.

Amendment XVI [1913]

The Congress shall have power to lay and collect taxes on incomes, from whatever source derived, without apportionment among the several States, and without regard to any census or enumeration.

Amendment XVII [1913]

The Senate of the United States shall be composed of two Senators from each State, elected by the people thereof, for six years; and each Senator shall have one vote. The electors in each State shall have the qualifications requisite for electors of the most numerous branch of the State legislatures.

When vacancies happen in the representation of any State in the Senate, the executive authority of such State shall issue writs of election to fill such vacancies: Provided, That the legislature of any State may empower the executive thereof to make temporary appointments until the people fill the vacancies by election as the legislature may direct.

This amendment shall not be so construed as to affect the election or term of any Senator chosen before it becomes valid as part of the Constitution.

Amendment XVIII [1919]

Section 1. After one year from the ratification of this article the manufacture, sale, or transportation of intoxicating liquors within, the importation thereof into, or the exportation thereof from the United States and all territory subject to the jurisdiction thereof for beverage purposes is hereby prohibited.

Section 2. The Congress and the several States shall have concurrent power to enforce this article by appropriate legislation.

Section 3. This article shall be inoperative unless it shall have been ratified as an amendment to the Constitution by the legislatures of the several States, as provided in the Constitution, within seven years from the date of the submission hereof to the States by the Congress.

Amendment XIX [1920]

The right of citizens of the United States to vote shall not be denied or abridged by the United States or by any State on account of sex.

Congress shall have power to enforce this article by appropriate legislation.

Amendment XX [1933]

Section 1. The terms of the President and Vice President shall end at noon on the 20th day of January, and the terms of Senators and Representatives at noon on the 3d day of January, of the years in which such terms would have ended if this article had not been ratified; and the terms of their successors shall then begin.

Section 2. The Congress shall assemble at least once in every year, and such meeting shall begin at noon on the 3d day of January, unless they shall by law appoint a different day.

Section 3. If, at the time fixed for the beginning of the term of the President, the President elect shall have died, the Vice President elect shall become President. If a President shall not have been chosen before the time fixed for the beginning of his term, or if the President elect shall have failed to qualify, then the Vice President elect shall act as President until a President shall have qualified; and the Congress may by law provide for the case wherein neither a President elect nor a Vice President elect shall have qualified, declaring who shall then act as President, or the manner in which one who is to act shall be selected, and such person shall act accordingly until a President or Vice President shall have qualified.

Section 4. The Congress may by law provide for the case of the death of any of the persons from whom the House of Representatives may choose a President whenever the right of choice shall have devolved upon them, and for the case of the death of any of the persons from whom the Senate may choose a Vice President whenever the right of choice shall have devolved upon them.

Section 5. Sections 1 and 2 shall take effect on the 15th day of October following the ratification of this article.

Section 6. This article shall be inoperative unless it shall have been ratified as an amendment to the Constitution by the legislatures of three-fourths of the several States within seven years from the date of its submission.

Amendment XXI [1933]

Section 1. The eighteenth article of amendment to the Constitution of the United States is hereby repealed.

Section 2. The transportation or importation into any State, Territory, or possession of the United States for delivery or use therein of intoxicating liquors, in violation of the laws thereof, is hereby prohibited.

Section 3. This article shall be inoperative unless it shall have been ratified as an amendment to the Constitution by conventions in the several States, as provided in the Constitution, within seven years from the date of the submission hereof to the States by the Congress.

Amendment XXII [1951]

Section 1. No person shall be elected to the office of the President more than twice, and no person who has held the office of President, or acted as President, for more than two years of a term to which some other person was elected President shall be elected to the office of the President more than once. But this Article shall not apply to any person holding the office of President when this Article was proposed by the Congress, and shall not prevent any person who may be holding the office of President, or acting as President, during the term within which this Article becomes operative from holding the office of President or acting as President during the remainder of such term.

Section 2. This article shall be inoperative unless it shall have been ratified as an amendment to the Constitution by the legislatures of three-fourths of the several States within seven years from the date of its submission to the States by the Congress.

Amendment XXIII [1961]

Section 1. The District constituting the seat of Government of the United States shall appoint in such manner as the Congress may direct:

A number of electors of President and Vice President equal to the whole number of Senators and Representatives in Congress to which the District would be entitled if it were a State, but in no event more than the least populous State; they shall be in addition to those appointed by the States, but they shall be considered, for the purposes of the election of President and Vice President, to be electors appointed by a State; and they shall meet in the District and perform such duties as provided by the twelfth article of amendment.

Section 2. The Congress shall have power to enforce this article by appropriate legislation.

Amendment XXIV [1964]

Section 1. The right of citizens of the United States to vote in any primary or other election for President or Vice President, for electors for President or Vice President, or for Senator or Representative in Congress, shall not be denied or abridged by the United States or any State by reason of failure to pay any poll tax or other tax.

Section 2. The Congress shall have power to enforce this article by appropriate legislation.

Amendment XXV [1967]

Section 1. In case of the removal of the President from office or of his death or resignation, the Vice President shall become President.

Section 2. Whenever there is a vacancy in the office of the Vice President, the President shall nominate a Vice President who shall take office upon confirmation by a majority vote of both Houses of Congress.

Section 3. Whenever the President transmits to the President pro tempore of the Senate and the Speaker of the House of Representatives his written declaration that he is unable to discharge the powers and duties of his office, and until he transmits to them a written declaration to the contrary, such powers and duties shall be discharged by the Vice President as Acting President.

Section 4. Whenever the Vice President and a majority of either the principal officers of the executive departments or of such other body as Congress may by law provide, transmit to the President pro tempore of the Senate and the Speaker of the House of Representatives their written declaration that the President is unable to discharge the powers and duties of his office, the Vice President shall immediately assume the powers and duties of the office as Acting President.

Thereafter, when the President transmits to the President pro tempore of the Senate and the Speaker of the House of Representatives his written declaration that no inability exists, he shall resume the powers and duties of his office unless the Vice President and a majority of either the principal officers of the executive department or of such other body as Congress may by law provide, transmit within four days to the President pro tempore of the Senate and the Speaker of the House of Representatives their written declaration that the President is unable to discharge the powers and duties of his office. Thereupon Congress shall decide the issue, assembling within forty-eight hours for that purpose if not in session. If the Congress, within twenty-one days after receipt of the latter written declaration, or, if Congress is not in session, within twenty-one days after Congress is required to assemble, determines by two-thirds vote of both Houses that the President is unable to discharge the powers and duties of his office, the Vice President shall continue to discharge the same as Acting President; otherwise, the President shall resume the powers and duties of his office.

Amendment XXVI [1971]

Section 1. The right of citizens of the United States, who are eighteen years of age or older, to vote shall not be denied or abridged by the United States or by any State on account of age.

Section 2. The Congress shall have power to enforce this article by appropriate legislation.

Amendment XXVII [1992]

No law, varying the compensation for the services of the Senators and Representatives, shall take effect, until an election of Representatives shall have intervened.

For Further Reading

Alderman, Ellen, and Caroline Kennedy. *In Our Defense: The Bill of Rights in Action*. New York: Morrow, 1991.

Amar, Akhil Reed. *America's Constitution: A Biography*. New York: Random House, 2005.

Baum, Lawrence. *The Supreme Court*. 9th Ed. Washington, D.C.: CQ Press, 2006.

Beveridge, Albert Jeremiah. *John Marshall*. New York: Chelsea House, 1980.

Breyer, Stephen G. *Active Liberty: Interpreting Our Democratic Constitution*. New York: Knopf, 2005.

Friendly, Fred W., and Martha J.H. Elliott. *The Constitution: That Delicate Balance*. New York: McGraw-Hill, 1993.

Garraty, John Arthur. *Quarrels That Have Shaped the Constitution*. New York: Harper & Row, 1964.

Hall, Kermit. *The Oxford Guide to United States Supreme Court Decisions*. New York: Oxford University Press, 1999.

Hartman, Gary R., Roy M. Mersky, and Cindy Tate. *Landmark Supreme Court Cases: The Most Influential Decisions of the Supreme Court of the United States*. New York: Facts on File, 2004.

Kluger, Richard. *Simple Justice: The History of Brown v. Board of Education and Black America's Struggle for Equality*. New York: Knopf, 1976.

Lewis, Anthony. *Gideon's Trumpet*. New York: Vintage Books, 1989.

Lewis, Thomas T., and Richard L. Wilson. *Encyclopedia of the U.S. Supreme Court*. Pasadena, Calif: Salem Press, 2001.

Mauro, Tony. *Illustrated Great Decisions of the Supreme Court*. Washington, D.C.: CQ Press, 2000.

McCloskey, Robert G., and Sanford Levinson. *The American Supreme Court*. 3rd Ed. Chicago: University of Chicago Press, 2000.

O'Connor, Sandra Day, and Craig Joyce. *The Majesty of the Law: Reflections of a Supreme Court Justice*. New York: Random House, 2003.

Rehnquist, William H. *The Supreme Court*. New York: Knopf, 2001.

Schwartz, Bernard. *A History of the Supreme Court*. New York: Oxford University Press, 1993.

Trachtman, Michael G. *The Supremes' Greatest Hits: The 34 Supreme Court Cases That Most Directly Affect Your Life*. New York: Sterling Pub., 2006.

Photo Credits

Photographs and illustrations reprinted with the permission of the following:
AP Images: p. 57
Arizona State Library, Archives and Public Records, Archives Division, Phoenix: p. 62 (97-7381)
Mark Ide, pp. 49, 51, 55, 61
iStockphoto.com: pp. cover, 5 (Jonathan Larsen), 79 (YinYang)
Public domain photographs and illustrations from the following:
Images of American Political History: p. 68
Gerald R. Ford Presidential Library and Museum: p. 70
Library of Congress: pp. 12, 20, 23, 25, 26, 29, 32, 34, 36, 39, 45,
Oyez: p. 58
U.S. National Archives & Records Administration: p. 72
White House: p. 85
Wikimedia Commons: pp. 16, 31, 74, 77
Wikipedia: pp. 18, 43, 87

Special Thanks to:

Michael Grimaldi
Ellen Hong
Kia Hudson

Table of Cases

Below are the titles of cases cited in the book followed by the legal citation, year, and the pages the cases are found in *Landmarks*.

Index